T0361671

Advance Praise for *American Impresario*

"All who came into Bill Buckley's orbit felt the magical pull of his friendship. In the last decade of Buckley's life, the pianist Larry Perelman grew especially close to him. This warm memoir of their friendship—enriched with the themes of immigration and exile, apprenticeship and self-discovery—imparts fresh magic of its own. I read it with admiration and pleasure."

- Sam Tanenhaus, Former Editor of
The New York Times Book Review

"*American Impresario* is a love letter—to a great man, William F. Buckley, Jr., who became the author's great friend, and to the great music, which provided so much of the stuff of their relationship. It is also a meditation on fealty—one of the virtues any of us, musical or not, can practice in this sad world."

- Richard Brookhiser, Author of *Glorious Lessons: John Trumbull: Painter of the American Revolution*

"*American Impresario* is a great read. I loved discovering the details of my friend Larry Perelman's earlier days. A young Jewish family with their talented sons escaping communist Russia finding refuge in this great country America, not unlike my coming to America as a young refugee at the age of twelve. It is evident in your dedication of *American Impresario* to William F. Buckley, Jr., that not only do you appreciate him as a mentor and music lover, but that the conservative values that Buckley professed; his fight against communism, anti-Semitism and his concern about civility, respect, and equality in the American fiber were his concern. Sentiments and values that you value and still relate to today."

- Lidia Bastianich

"Larry Perelman has written an affecting memoir of his deep friendship with one of the great figures of the 20th Century, united by their love of the finest music ever composed and of the high points of our civilization."

- Rich Lowry, Editor in Chief, *National Review*

AMERICAN IMPRESARIO

*William F. Buckley, Jr., and the
Elements of American Character*

LAWRENCE PERELMAN

BOMBARDIER
BOOKS

Published by Bombardier Books
An Imprint of Post Hill Press
ISBN: 979-8-88845-379-7
ISBN (eBook): 979-8-88845-380-3

American Impresario:
William F. Buckley, Jr., and the Elements of American Character
© 2025 by Lawrence Perelman
All Rights Reserved

Cover Design by Jim Villaflores

The image on the cover of the book was taken by photographer Ken Regan on October 3, 1972, Firing Line (Television program) broadcast records, Box 8, Folder 1, Hoover Institution Library & Archives.

Page 99 "Is Good Music Going Under?", [Identification of item], Firing Line (Television program) broadcast records, box 146, Folder 15, Hoover Institution Library & Archives.

Page 124 "Is Good Music Going Under?", [Identification of item], Firing Line (Television program) broadcast records, box 146, Folder 15, Hoover Institution Library & Archives.

Page 88 "A Musical Question: To Perform or Not Perform?", [Identification of item], Firing Line (Television program) broadcast records, box 124, Folder 19, Hoover Institution Library & Archives.

This book, as well as any other Bombardier Books publications, may be purchased in bulk quantities at a special discounted rate. Contact orders@bombardierbooks.com for more information.

This is a work of nonfiction. All people, locations, events, and situations are portrayed to the best of the author's memory.

No part of this book may be reproduced, stored in a retrieval system, or transmitted by any means without the written permission of the author and publisher.

BOMBARDIER
BOOKS

Post Hill
PRESS

Post Hill Press
New York • Nashville
posthillpress.com

Published in the United States of America
1 2 3 4 5 6 7 8 9 10

To Mom and Dad, the people who gave me life;
My brother Rubin for always being there for me;
&
My wife Anna and our children Elizabeth and
Gabriella for being my life and loves.

Contents

William F. Buckley, Jr. playing his Bösendorfer piano at the maisonette located at 73 East 73rd Street in New York. Photograph by Jan Lukas. Date Unknown. Courtesy of Christopher Buckley.

Prologue

I toyed many times with the idea of writing a book about my friendship with William F. Buckley, Jr. (1925–2008) but never thought it would become a reality. When my editor David Bernstein said he was interested, I was taken aback. I'm humbled to give readers a front row seat to some of my experiences, recollections, and thoughts about this great man who became my friend, Bill.

When I began writing this book, the task at hand was daunting, yet also somewhat familiar. I knew Bill Buckley very well, but researching this book brought me closer to him and made me value him even more. My friendship with him began when I wrote him a letter. He wrote back. We met. We became friends. Well, it's not that simple, but at its essence, it is.

I was nineteen, a first-generation American studying to be a concert pianist, when Bill and I met in April 1995. The door opening to his Manhattan maisonette was a Narnian experience. Behind that door was the New York City I only knew about from movies, magazines, and books. It was a magisterial place where someone who would come to believe in me and celebrate my talents lived. An extraordinary cross-generational and cross-religious friendship blossomed at just the right moment for us both.

I have three goals for this book. (1) Tell the story about my friendship with William F. Buckley, Jr., which reflects the American Dream. (2) Impart what I believe Bill did for our nation as an American impresario, by focusing on his battles against Communism and anti-Semitism. (3) Inspire those reading this book to emulate Buckley's virtues to help to transform our society for the better.

The following chapters present a dual story; my take on how Bill attained his skills to become an American impresario, and the story of our friendship which was sparked by a common passion for classical music. The power of this story is generated from the lessons I learned from his character and that which he bestowed upon me through his friendship, mentorship, time, generosity, and other virtues, all of which set me on a path I continue to travel to this day.

William F. Buckley, Jr. and the author following the
taping of the final episode of *Firing Line* on December
19, 1999. Courtesy of Lawrence Perelman.

Chapter 1

THE DIABELLI VARIATIONS: FEBRUARY 19, 2008

The Diabelli Variations by Ludwig van Beethoven is a wretchedly difficult work and maddening to assemble but as I neared the finish line it began to make sense. Here was Beethoven telling the story of his life through the transformation of a simple little waltz by a publisher, not a fellow composer of note. Through this work one travels the entire spectrum of Beethoven from classical to romantic and then to a cosmic and celestial Beethoven, which takes one to the outer reaches of the human mind's capabilities. The work is physically demanding at nearly an hour and, unlike the Goldberg Variations, where Johann Sebastian Bach brings back the aria at the very end, Beethoven fades away with the thirty-third and final variation, like a comet disappearing into the cosmos.

On February 16, 2008, I received an urgent email from Bill, "Larry must talk with you but can't find your phone number. Please call me...xxb." I called him and to my surprise he asked me to come to Wallacks Point (his home in Stamford,

1

Connecticut) in a few days to play Beethoven's magnum opus which he simply referred to as, "the Diabelli," in his quintessential accent. He had to confirm a few things but said it looked like it would be Tuesday, February 19. I told him my mom was visiting and he said she was absolutely welcome.

On Sunday, February 17, Bill wrote, "Larry, tried to reach you by phone. Ok Diabelli on Tuesday [February 19]. I will have Jerry pick you and your mama up at 10:30 [a.m.] and returned after lunch. Just give me an address and confirm receipt of this. xxb." It was really happening! I was going to tackle the Diabelli for Bill. "Hi Bill, This is GREAT!" I provided my address for his driver Jerry and closed with, "We're looking forward to this! "This performance was initiated on the phone without the knowledge of Linda Bridges, a longtime *National Review* editor who now looked after Bill's logistics and social diary. She chimed in, having eyes on Bill's emails and reconfirmed everything with Jerry, so he had our coordinates, and we were set.

This last-minute production was Bill, the impresario, in action. The invitation was completely unforeseen. I didn't know whom to expect. But it didn't matter who was in the audience, I had to keep practicing and ironing out the final potholes in the Diabelli, and there were many in this massive work. I was reluctant to tackle this piece even though Bill had brought it up repeatedly during our friendship where music was the nexus point.

Mom and I waited outside my apartment building on 84th Street near West End Avenue. Up drove Bill's limousine at exactly 10:30 a.m. Jerry opened the door for Mom and me. Off we drove to Stamford. Mom couldn't believe this was happening, nor could I. My performances always made Mom nervous, but this was different. She had never attended one of my recitals at the maisonette and hadn't seen Bill since his eightieth birthday in 2005. I was nervous with excitement and just couldn't wait to give Bill this gift on which I had been working for about nine months. Learning a piece of music does require a gestational period and needs to settle in one's mind in order to be born. Therefore, nine months for the Diabelli was just about right but, honestly, one can work on it for a lifetime and keep finding new things.

We drove along the now familiar driveway passing the barn, which served as Bill's office, just yards away from the house. Jerry pulled up, stepped out of the car and opened the door for us. We got out and at the door was Bill. He was definitely more haggard, after his wife Pat's passing and various health issues. Nevertheless, I saw the Bill I had known since 1995. I re-introduced Mom to Bill and she was absolutely beaming, as was he. It turned out the audience for this recital were the remaining Buckley siblings save for Reid Buckley, who lived in South Carolina. Of the ten Buckley siblings those present were Bill, Priscilla, Trish (Patricia Bozell), and Jim Buckley, the former senator from New York and former federal judge nominated by President Reagen to the US Court of Appeals for the District of Columbia, as well as Carol, a cousin from Texas. I had met Priscilla many times over the years and she, as a member of *National Review*'s staff, had heard nearly all of my recitals at the glorious Buckley maisonette located at 73 East 73rd Street in Manhattan. The others, I had never met before. We had a wonderful conversation in the music room overlooking the Long Island Sound. This room was home to the harpsichord while the Bösendorfer piano selected for Bill by the legendary harpsichordist and pianist Rosalyn Tureck was in the living room. Bill sat with his oxygen machine whirling throughout the conversation, but after a few minutes, one didn't notice it. He spoke with difficulty but definitively.

We made our way to the living room and Bill required some help to move. He took a few steps at a time and seemed to have gained some weight. It turned out that a medication he was on led to bloating causing him to slow down considerably since I last saw him. Everyone took their seats and I recounted the adventure taken to get to this afternoon along with my reluctance to learn the Diabelli. I told the story of how, when Bill had initially selected the Diabelli in April 2007, my reply was "I hate the Diabelli." I then recounted how I offered Bill the Liszt B minor sonata only to have him reply, "I hate the Liszt sonata." "We were at a standstill and we made a compromise. I learned the Diabelli." Everyone laughed. It was a real family gathering and such an honor to play for them. The Wallacks Point Bösendorfer was only a few decades old, so as an instrument it was much more manageable and also more compact at about six-feet than the eight-foot thousand-pound Bösendorfer in Manhattan which dated from 1927. I gave every ounce of myself in this performance thinking of Bill and the years of recitals and all the memoires. Each one of those performances had built up to this hour. Having Mom present was particularly poignant. Giving her an afternoon in this magical place was also a present to her for everything she had done from birth to bring music into my life.

That afternoon, Bill had managed to replicate for his siblings the experiences they had shared at their home Great Elm in Sharon, Connecticut more than seventy years ago. The performance went by in a flash and before I knew it the final notes of the thirty-third variation had dissipated. The room was tremendously warm with joy and everyone could sense the special bond we had through music that afternoon. Bill was gleeful and I gave him a big hug. Mom would later tell me how Bill sat behind me and reacted with amazement at each challenging bar of music. He was always the most involved member of the audience.

We all moved to the dining room where the table was set beautifully. Julian, Bill and Pat's longtime chef, was present and oversaw every detail. Bill sat Mom next to him, and Trish sat on one side of me and Priscilla on the other. There's a snapshot in my mind's eye of that glowing room and how everyone looked. For the next hour we dined, reminisced, spoke of music and a little bit of politics. It was a delight to be in their company. The light of the afternoon gave an otherworldly glint to the room. It turned out that these Buckley children would be dining together for the last time. Trish, who was roommates with Pat at Vassar and responsible for Bill and Pat meeting, told me about a play, *33 Variations*, which she had seen in Washington, DC. She invited me to come down anytime to see it and to play her piano. Alas, I never made it. She made a powerful impression that first and only time we met. There was a saintliness to her, especially in that light. Jim and Priscilla resided at Great Elm, and they invited me to come play for them anytime, an offer I would take up in the future.

After dessert, Mom and I bid everyone farewell and Bill mentioned he couldn't wait for me to come back the next week on February 27 to play the Diabelli again for some friends. Mom and I thanked him again, gave him a hug, and headed back to the car.

As Jerry drove us back to the Upper West Side, I bottled that afternoon into my mind's cellar. Mom began to cry. I was in denial about Bill's state of health. Mom knew what was coming. I was blinded by the brightness of the spirit at Wallacks Point and our friendship. I didn't think about the physical deterioration he had undergone and still saw the Bill who first greeted me at the maisonette's door thirteen years earlier. Mom didn't say anything as I consoled her.

The next morning, the buzzer in my apartment rang. It was a delivery: A bouquet of flowers from Bill with a note, "You were sensational and I love your mother." The floral arrangement was tremendous with several dozen flowers of various types. Mom immediately confiscated the note and said, "this is mine!" The note is framed in Minnesota. "Dear Bill," I wrote that afternoon, "First of all, thank you for the incredible floral arrangement. Wow! It is magnificent. Your note was so kind and Mom was so very touched. It was a tremendous honor for me to not only play for your family but to be a part of a very special morning and afternoon. Thank you." I continued:

> My mom had a wonderful time and enjoyed meeting everyone. She cherished the time with you and will convey everything to my dad who sends you his warmest wishes. I assume we are still on for next Tuesday, February 26 and Wednesday, February 27. I think the plan was for me to head out to Stamford in the afternoon on Feb. 26 and spend the night. I would then play in the evening of the 27th and either head back to the City in the evening or the next morning, the 28th.

I closed with: "Please confirm this when you have a moment and know that whenever you need some Diabelli…I'm there! I wish you well in every respect and thank you so much for being a part of my life. Love, Larry."

Linda Bridges confirmed the plan. She added in a post-script, "By the way, I just heard from Trish Bozell—you made a big hit with her, and she is probably (I think Bill would agree) the most musical member of the family." I was overjoyed and couldn't wait to return to Wallacks Point on February 26.

Chapter 2

FROM GREAT ELM TO PARK AVENUE

The formative years of William F. Buckley, Jr.'s life were forged at Great Elm, the estate in Sharon, Connecticut, built by his father William F. Buckley, Sr., an oilman lawyer who lost one fortune in Mexico only to make another one there and then expanded to Venezuela. For Bill and his nine siblings the sound of music, especially classical music, was ingrained early on, leading most of them to become lifelong classical music enthusiasts. Bill and his sister Patricia (Trish) were the most serious, so much so that they contemplated careers as musicians. Bill even devised a new notation system for the keyboard published in 1994 titled *Getting Back to the Piano: Of Course You Can Play! Featuring William F. Buckley Jr.'s New Notation System*. This quirky volume—now out of print—shows just how passionate he was about the instrument and encouraging people to learn it at any age.

The Buckley children—who were tutored at home through grade eight and then sent to boarding school—were all required to play the piano, which included weekly private lessons and practice sessions with a teacher who would over three days give lessons on five pianos across the sprawling estate. In addition to these lessons the Buckley children each had to practice forty-five minutes a day, which Bill described in his memoir *Miles Gone By*: "It was never absolutely clear whether the sound was worse when all the pianos were being exercised jointly or when only one of them was being played." In addition, the children were required to attend listening sessions of great works of music curated by Penelope Oyen, one of the children's tutors. Bill wrote in the same memoir that "Miss Oyen loved music with passion. The use of that word here is not platitudinous. Because Penelope Oyen would *weep* when listening to music. Not always, not for every composer; but almost always for J.S. Bach." Her influence on the children was such that these lessons along with the listening sessions, in Bill's opinion, led to the children's appetite for classical music:

> The drill was four times a week. At four o'clock we came in from afternoon recreation and entered The Playroom, as we inaccurately continued out of habit to call the room over which Miss Oyen now had dominion. My father had bought a huge phonograph, a Capehart, which, if memory serves, was the first instrument that boasted that it could handle records consecutively. This it did, not by the simple device of dropping a fresh record on the one just finished, but by actually taking the record, when finished, and convolutedly lifting it up, turning it around, and either placing its backside on the turntable, or replacing it with the next record,

a quite remarkable feat of engineering executed at the cost of a broken record every two or three days; expensive fractures which, however, had as an uncharted social benefit the interruption of Miss Oyen's lacrimations.

The absolutely decisive feature of Miss Oyen's discipline was very simple: darkness in the room. Not total darkness, else we'd have ended up playing Sardines. Too much light, and we'd have managed to read—anything, anything to avoid just…sitting there, listening to what I suppose in those days we'd have called "that darned music." There was simply no escaping it. We just sat there, while the Capehart blared away, and the ordeal lasted one whole hour.

And, of course…it happened. I'd say it took, depending on the individual child's latent inclinations, between four and eight months. My oldest brother, John (RIP), was ejected from our tutorial system in the fifth month to go to boarding school, and the result was that he never ever got around to enjoying beautiful music. I am willing to bet that if he had stayed with Miss Oyen another two months, he'd have become an addict, which is what happened to the rest of us.

Bill recognized in his teens that he lacked the requisite talent to pursue a career as a professional musician but his love of music was formed and was quite possibly only surpassed by his reverence for the divine.

Decades later as Bill hosted *Firing Line* he would often promulgate classical music's importance to him and humanity, since to him it was one of the major achievements of our civilization. Any excuse to bring up Bach was taken, most notably with the *Firing Line* "jingle" for many seasons, which in conservative circles became iconic: the opening of the third movement of Bach's Brandenburg Concerto No. 2. It turns out that Bill wrote a paper on this concerto during his studies at Yale, so when time came to select a theme for *Firing Line*, a lifelong favorite was naturally the one. Bach was divine for Bill as illustrated by the following excerpt from a column dedicated to Bach's 300th birthday in 1985 in the book *Happy Days Were Here Again*:

> It is not necessary to believe in God in order to revel in Bach. It is not necessary, for that matter, to love one's country in order to fight for it, nor even to love one's family in order to protect it. And there is no need to make heavy weather over the point, though there is a need for such human modesty as Einstein expressed when he said that the universe was not explicable except by the acknowledgment of an unknown mover. The music of Bach disturbs human complacency because one can't readily understand finiteness in its presence.

When looking back at the Buckley era from the 1950s to early 2000s, we can see that faith and music were central. As founder and editor of *National Review*, Bill played the role of impresario and hosted fortnightly dinners at his maisonette on 73rd and Park Avenue for decades. Those dinners were events in Buckley circles with standing invitations for the editors of *National Review* and then spillover to friends of Bill and his wife Patricia T. Buckley, one of New York's preeminent socialites, including guests of honor ranging from writers to politicians, musicians, and clergy. Music would often play a role at these dinners with classical pianists and harpsichordists, from amateurs to professionals, performing Bach, Beethoven, Chopin, Schubert, and, on rarer occasions, jazz pianists. Bill aimed to convert those that weren't musically attuned through these performances, which preceded dinner, where the political discussions would take place often culminating in a mock *Firing Line* with by-now-inebriated participants.

The fact that music played a central role in the impresario's dinner parties harkens back to those hour-long listening sessions at Great Elm. Just as Bill was convinced that his brother John would have become an aficionado of great music had he only participated in Miss Oyen's listening sessions for a few more months, Bill was similarly convinced that he could convert to classical music lovers the uninitiated listeners after repeated interpretations of Bach and Beethoven.

It was a long way from Great Elm to Park Avenue but the values instilled in Bill in a home of ten children gave him the tools to manage and lead a movement, found a magazine, host a television program, and become the impresario of the conservative movement which ultimately led to the defeat of the Soviet Union. Bill was the architect of the conservative movement and his designs were the example on which so many others were based. He made conservatism cool and fun. He made conservatism commercially viable. He made conservatism charismatic and compelling. Without his mold the conservative movement might have sputtered and not spawned dozens of publications, television programs, networks, and foundations, and not built a movement out of the commonalities of different philosophical and ideological strands. I'm speaking of the conservatism of the 1980s through early 2010s, but even in the past decade where the definition of conservatism has become less clear, there are elements of Bill's influence that remain, and many leaders still clearly revere him.

In my experience, Bill had two favorite composers: Bach and Beethoven. However, if he had to choose one it would have been Johann Sebastian Bach. There are some parallels between the two. Where Bill had nine siblings, Bach had seven. Bill was a devout Christian, as was Bach. At the time of his passing, Bill had more than 1,500 episodes of *Firing Line*; 1,100 boxes of correspondence sent to the Yale archive, fifty-five books, and thousands of columns. At the time of his passing, Bach left more than 1,100 works of music. Bill was the most important conservative in history and from whom all others would blossom. Bach was the most important composer in history, from whom all others would blossom.

At the time of Bach's passing he was remembered as an organist, not as a composer. Bill was remembered more for his television program and founding of *National Review* than for his writings, which included thousands of articles and his books, most famously his first, *God and Man at Yale*. That book is more relevant today than ever before as the campus wars have compounded, core Western values continue to dissipate at our nation's leading colleges and universities, and anti-Semitism has become a major issue. Bill also presciently wrote of anti-Semitism, dedicating an entire issue of *National Review* to the topic in the 1990s and ultimately turning it into the book *In Search of Anti-Semitism*.

In another excerpt from the column published on Bach's 300th birthday, Bill writes:

> There are sobering lessons to contemplate on Bach's birthday. One of them is that when he lived he was almost entirely unnoticed. True, he was renowned as a virtuoso at the harpsichord and the organ. When he died, one of his biographers notes, there were something on the order of ninety obituaries written, only three of which, however, mentioned him as a composer. This is tantamount to remembering Shakespeare as a great actor.

When Bill passed away he, too, was the subject of countless obituaries including on the frontpages of the nation's most important newspapers, including *The New York Times* and *The Washington Post*, as well as the lead item on many of the nation's newscasts. However, as we near twenty years since his passing, the public's memory of Bill is fading with the natural ebbs and flows of the tide as it washes away the beach and makes way for the new sand. This isn't to say that Bill is yet as forgotten as Bach was decades after his death, only to be rediscovered by Felix Mendelssohn. Bill is the subject of films and plays, yet this is still niche compared to where he was in life when the media landscape was much less fractured.

The goal of these pages is to shine a light on the importance of Bill the impresario and how that role was actually where we as a society can still learn from him. He was the impresario who brought together people and was friends with those of different stripes. As a mentor he was the great connector always bringing people together and letting the sparks take on a life of their own.

As we wander in this age of uncertainty we should look to Bill as an example of what to emulate. My small place in his life gave me a vantage point after I wrote him a letter thirty years ago and he decided to answer it. As a first-generation American, I am eternally grateful to Bill for his contributions to this nation and for creating an environment in which new Americans, like my family, were able to flourish. The following pages tell the story of my family's journey to this nation, my ambition to become a pianist and classical music impresario, and how Bill became a central figure in my life.

William F. Buckley, Jr.'s role in our nation's history was tremendously consequential, and I hope that my perspective on and friendship with this giant, this mentor, this American impresario of the twentieth century, will serve as an example to many and help to improve the state of our society.

Chapter 3

IMPRESARIO

Merriam-Webster's definition of Impresario:

Impresario **noun**

im·pre·sa·rio -ˈser-, -ˈzär-

1: the promoter, manager, or conductor of an opera or concert company

2: a person who puts on or sponsors an entertainment (such as a television show or sports event)

3: MANAGER, DIRECTOR

English borrowed *impresario* directly from Italian, whose noun *impresa* means "undertaking." A close relative is the English word emprise ("an adventurous, daring, or chivalric enterprise"), which, like *impresario*, traces back to the Latin verb *prehendere*, meaning "to seize." (That verb is also the source of apprehend, comprehend, and prehensile.)

E ach of the three definitions above applies to William F. Buckley, Jr. He was the ultimate "promoter" for American conservatism; "put on" or produced *Firing Line*, his television show; and was the "manager" or "director" of his magazine *National Review*. He understood that American conservatism had to be entertaining to attract an audience, but more than anything he understood the need to harmonize the various strands that made up conservatism by removing those that created dissonance, such as anti-Semites and the John Birch Society, among other fringe groups. His work was not unlike that of a great maestro who is responsible for keeping an orchestra playing together and with momentum so that the audience is emotionally moved by the performance.

Where did Bill hone the skills that made him an incredible polymath or was it simply talent that he possessed as part of his DNA? As mapped out in the previous chapter, Bill was raised in the rarified environment of Great Elm where music was a centerpiece of his life along with faith. My theory is that the countless hours spent practicing piano as a child along with listening to classical music with his siblings four times a week played a major role in giving Bill an incredible amount of disciple along with enhancing his ability to speak and write melodiously, as a musician plays, sings, or composes a score. Bill's prose was musical, and colleagues have commented on how words flowed from his fingers on a keyboard or typewriter much like musical notation flowed from Mozart's mind, where it was already complete and edited, onto a score.

Bill, the impresario, also produced countless recitals at his home on East 73rd Street in Manhattan, where he many times selected the masterworks performed by his musician friends and acquaintances. His aim was to shine a light on Bach, Beethoven, and other composers, for his *National Review* editors as well as his friends. His hope, I believe, was to evangelize on the beauty of music he loved for both the initiated and uninitiated, just as Miss Oyen had done at Great Elm. In this environment, Bill created the ultimate salon where the exchange of ideas was of paramount importance during dinner parties where guests spanned the ideological spectrum. This salon was not unlike the family dinner table where Bill was often at odds with his siblings in the endless debates they had growing up.

Bill further built upon these salons at his home as the ringmaster of *Firing Line*, the longest-running public affairs program with a single host in American history. He hosted more than 1,500 episodes featuring guests from every walk of life and every cultural sphere, including those to whom he was diametrically opposed ideologically, culturally, and spiritually. His hundreds upon hundreds of guests ranged from Beat poet Allen Ginsburg to Muhammad Ali, Richard Nixon to Ronald Reagan, Tom Wolfe to Norman Mailer, as well as the pianist Rosalyn Tureck on whom Bill often called to remind his audience of Bach's importance to the broader culture. The program was an open forum for debate where nearly every idea was welcome. *Firing Line*'s impact on the cultural fabric was keenly felt from 1966 until 1999. This program was also an extension of the childhood dinner table at Great Elm. He had his father's affection not only as his namesake but also for the stances he took and his ability to defend his positions.

Bill's abilities as an impresario allowed him to bring together the intellectual giants representing various strands of conservatism in *National Review*'s formative years, including James Burnham, Russell Kirk, Willmoore Kendall, and Frank Meyer. All of these gentlemen were Bill's seniors, with Kendall a mentor at Yale. Although Bill doesn't literally refer to Willi Schlamm as a mentor, it was in fact this Austrian-American Jewish ex-Communist, who fled the Nazis in 1941, who lit the spark that inspired Bill, as he wrote in his memoir *Miles Gone By*, to

> launch a weekly conservative journal of opinion, by which he [Schlamm] meant nothing less than that I should raise the capital for it, own the voting stock, and serve as editor in chief. These suggestions issued not out of any recognition of precocious talents (I was twenty-eight), but out of a conviction that my youth would prove precisely the catalytic agent, and I think Willi was correct in this.

Bill continues, "I doubt that, if I had been twenty years older, I'd have succeeded in engaging the attention, let alone collaboration, of the starting team at *National Review*, whom with the exception of Willmoore Kendall, I didn't know well, certainly not intimately."

Bill and Schlamm had different visions for *National Review*, and Schlamm had a reputation for quickly wearing out his welcome at publications, including as a right hand to the legendary Henry Luce at *Time*. Schlamm seemed to assume that he would have unparalleled influence over Bill at *National Review* due to his formative role. This early relationship was rife with generational tensions one could have expected from an émigré mentor like Schlamm, twenty years his protégé's senior. It took five years for a permanent parting of ways and they barely spoke after, but the fact that Bill included Schlamm in a chapter titled "Five Colleagues" in his memoir, confirms for me that this relationship was one of the most important in Bill's entire life. The fact that Schlamm was Jewish further illustrates the importance of Jews in Bill's life. As the impresario of the American conservative movement, its producer and provocateur, it was Bill who represented its values and set the key goals and tenets which placed the defeat of the hegemonic evil of Communism at its core along with forbidding the appearance of anti-Semitism within *his* conservative coalition.

Bill's anti-Communism is what drew my family into his intellectual orbit as my parents discovered *Firing Line* not long after emigrating to America in 1975. Growing up in the 1980s, I learned that Bill was not only an anti-Communist warrior but led a valiant fight against anti-Semitism. Bill's anti-Communism, along with his efforts to confront anti-Semitism head on, made him a heroic figure for me and untold others. Not only was Bill the impresario who built the modern conservative movement, but someone who defended its borders from extremists. Revisionist history is rampant in our society both on the Left and the Right. The most high-profile biographical documentary produced since his death in 2008 is "The Incomparable Mr. Buckley," broadcast on PBS in 2024. It contained some very touching family photos, archival films, and interviews with his son Christopher, along with a few other close colleagues including Richard Brookhiser, Lee Edwards, and Jay Nordlinger. The film was roundly criticized in conservative circles for focusing on fleeting moments of controversy, and for not being clearer that Bill's positions evolved over time, including *National Review*'s initial opposition to the 1964 Civil Rights Act. The film also speculates about what Bill would make of the conservative coalition since his death in 2008, especially since 2016, and even veers into suggesting that he was in some way responsible for unleashing the most venomous elements seen on the Right. What the film did *not* mention was his battle against anti-Semitism and glossed over the magnitude of his achievements related to anti-Communism and the collapse of the Soviet Union.

Bill was also one of the most consequential Catholics of his lifetime but I never felt that he proselytized. If anything, he avoided overtly speaking about the details of Catholicism when in the presence of, as he would say, "non-believers." Of course, there was the presence of a priest, here and there, most often Father George W. Rutler, who presided over Bill's memorial Mass at St. Patrick's Cathedral in New York. Even as a Jew I felt something special to be in the presence of believers of other faiths, in this case Catholicism. Many of the editors at *National Review* were religious but came from different denominations. There were also converts, here and there, with the most notable being Larry Kudlow who converted to Catholicism after battling drug addiction. There was a unity and humanity amongst friends of Bill and an understanding that Bill was the most devout among them. Bill, until his dying day, preferred his Mass in Latin even after the Second Vatican Council forbade it. Something about this always stood out for me in that Bill was a man of tradition and seeing these traditions decay caused him disappointment and made him rebel against the rebellion. Not for nothing, *National Review*'s founding motto was "Standing Athwart History Yelling Stop!"

In 1991, an issue of *National Review* arrived in my parents' mailbox. It was dedicated to a single article by Bill: "In Search of Anti-Semitism." This was Bill's treatise on the state of anti-Semitism in America and the worrying potential of its rise in the conservative movement if left unchecked. Here was one America's foremost Catholics taking a stand on behalf of not only Jews but all Americans. Although he had evicted the anti-Semites and conspiracy theorists from his conservative movement decades earlier, Bill knew that his work wasn't finished, warning that the weeds were growing back into the post-Cold War conservative movement. This monumental work was his conscious retort to those who might have thought that his blend of conservatism would enable the centuries-old smears of anti-Semitism to persist. Reading this in *National Review* further solidified Bill's position in my mind. His honesty about his childhood was particularly raw and heartening when he recalled that in 1937 several of his siblings along with a few neighborhood friends in Sharon, Connecticut, decided to burn a cross in front of a Jewish resort not far from Great Elm. Bill goes as far as to point out that John Judis, his early biographer, confirmed that Bill was not among the group, yet Bill admits what Judis doesn't mention, that Bill actually "wept" at being left behind from the group because he was too young to participate at age eleven. This kind of unvarnished honesty paints a picture of the anti-Semitism that existed around Bill—promulgated by his father and others in his family—and that he aimed to repent for it and to fight it.

Bill's evolution into a crusader against anti-Semitism is part and parcel of what made him an American impresario. He used his perch to shine a light on the festering scourge of anti-Semitism and call those out who traded in it. We are now living through an era where apologists for rampant anti-Semitism hide in plain sight without taking a demonstrative stance to rid the political landscape of this scourge. Bill didn't hide, he put it on the cover of his magazine!

One can clearly see that Bill's anti-Communism and crusade against anti-Semitism went hand in hand. He plowed the way forward for the Soviet Jewry that made its permanent exodus from the evils of the Soviet Union and then further saw to it, inasmuch as he was able, that the terrain on which it tread was cleared of the venomous anti-Semitism from which its members fled in the first place. This attitude allowed him to become colleagues with Willi Schlamm, which led to the creation of *National Review* itself.

When I began writing this book in the summer of 2023, the flames of anti-Semitism were being stoked by a relatively small group across the political sphere. Then came October 7, 2023, and anti-Semitism began to rage throughout America, on its foremost college campuses, and around the world. The loss of a voice of reason like Bill's is felt most at a time like this. His humanity was evident through his faith and a drive to connect with his fellow human beings by doing right, communicating emphatically yet elegantly, and by driving out those whom he saw as troublemakers. I was just fifteen when that issue of *National Review* arrived, but the starkness of the font and title on the magazine's cover and the act of dedicating the entire issue to anti-Semitism, was proof of the depth and courage that Bill possessed along with his humanity and faith.

Bill ultimately went on to expand the article "In Search of Anti-Semitism" into a book of the same title in 1993. I sent my first letter to him in September 1994, so the topic of anti-Semitism wasn't too far from his mind. To draw a through line from his writings on anti-Semitism to my becoming a protégé is perhaps a stretch. However, I'm willing to stretch it since this is my book. The fact is that there was a day in the fall of 1994 when William F. Buckley, Jr., sat at his desk in New York and read my letter, the letter of the son of Soviet Jewish immigrants, offering to play a recital for him as a thank you present for his great deeds. He would not only invite me to his Upper East Side home to play that recital, but three years later, when I wrote to him again, he would offer me a grant and, with it, entry into his extraordinary world as his protégé.

Impresarios are those who bring to fruition worlds that to others are illusory. They are producers of concerts and television programs and creators of publications. They are also the producers of nations. The founding fathers were impresarios in this respect, with the Constitution being their vision for a nation. Over the past two and a half centuries, politicians and judges have interpreted this document to shape the lives of the American citizenry, essentially interpreting the text as an actor would lines from a play. Bill's imprint on the nation was tremendous and led to the election of Ronald Reagan, the halcyon days of the 1980s, and ultimately the demise of the Soviet Union. If one wants to write about a through line, that is the one. That was his vision as the American impresario, to see a day when those enslaved to Communism would be released from their chains. He also resolved to unmask the creeping venom of anti-Semitism and to rid it from conservatism's borders. What we lack today are more American impresarios of the Buckley mold, serving the interests of this nation and its greatest values rather than themselves. If we had more of them, our fight against anti-Semitism would be more successful and far more lasting.

Chapter 4

FROM MOSCOW TO MINNESOTA

The 1980s are most certainly the decade in which Communism ceased to be a creed, surviving only as a threat. And Ronald Reagan had more to do with this than any other statesman in the world.

—WILLIAM F. BUCKLEY, JR., *THE REAGAN I KNEW*

G rowing up in St. Paul, Minnesota, in the 1980s was as Midwest as Midwest could be. Our modest house in a middle-class neighborhood of Highland Park was just a block from the Mississippi River. Neighborhood kids were friendly and played with each other, and families knew one another well. During the long winters my brother Rubin, seven years my senior, and his friends would set up mock hockey rinks in backyards by filling up lawns with water. Minnesota was hockey country, after all. This ruined more than one lawn but the fun of it still shines through in my memory. Nostalgia is in the eye of the beholder, but as I get older, I begin to see that this was a much more genuine time than we live in today. Neighbors might not have agreed on all things politics or religion but things weren't aired as bluntly as they are today where, due to social media, almost everyone knows everyone's opinions on everything. People seemed to have kept to the old rules of no politics or religion among friends or work colleagues unless absolutely certain of someone's affiliation, and even then, one would tread lightly.

There were ruffles in the feathers though and things could bubble up in the form of childhood taunting of one another. I must have been about ten or eleven when I fell off my bike in a neighbor's backyard and the younger sister said, "That's what happens to people who don't believe in Jesus." What? That was new. I had never encountered anything like it. I went home and told my parents. Was this anti-Semitism? My mom called the girl's mother, who was shocked, and couldn't understand where her daughter could have heard such a thing. Regardless, her parents made her apologize and we continued on our way with fun-filled summer days. This didn't become anything more than a blip because we found a civilized way to deal with it. We dealt with it directly and personally, not through a bull horn that would destroy; there weren't any virtual bullhorns in the late 1980s. More than thirty-five years later I look at this incident and wonder what would have happened today in our hyperpolarized and reactionary world. Would we have been direct with our neighbor and discussed the incident or made it fodder for social media and shaming of a family? I don't know, but the character of our nation today definitely points in the direction of a knee-jerk reaction to shame someone instead of having a talk. The importance of communicating with one another openly was palpable from my perspective growing up. Both of my parents spoke with discernible accents but we rarely encountered discrimination based on that. There was an acceptance of immigrants in our community with Minnesota often leading the way for enthusiastically opening its doors to people from war-torn and Communist countries, such as Vietnam, Cambodia, and the USSR in the 1970s and 1980s, and, more recently, Somalia.

My parents and brother left the Soviet Union in 1975. The opportunities in 1975 for Mom aged twenty-eight, and Dad aged thirty-three, were limited at best. Rubin at age six was looking at a dim future had they not left the Soviet Union and could have been sent to fight in Afghanistan in the 1980s. Hundreds of thousands of Soviet Jews emigrated to America from the mid-1960s until the fall of the Soviet Union in 1991. The real exodus began in the 1970s when Scoop Jackson, the anti-Communist senator from Washington State, spearheaded the efforts for Soviet Jewry to initially make it to Israel through the Jackson-Vanik amendment to the Trade Act of 1974, which required countries with non-market economies to guarantee freedom of movement for Jews if those countries wanted to do business with the US. The first beneficiary of the Jackson-Vanik amendment in our family was my father's cousin Vlad and his family who left Moscow in 1974. Once he and his family made it to St. Paul in 1974, the odds for my parents went up. Vlad, his wife Tanya, and son Michael traveled from Moscow to Vienna, as was the case for Soviet Jews routed to Israel. However, Vlad wanted to make in America. He died in 2019 and would often tell the tale of how he walked out of a monastery in Vienna, where his refugee group was housed, and found a Hebrew Immigrant Aid Society (HIAS) office. HIAS sent Vlad and his family to Italy, where they awaited their papers, and then to America. My parents, along with tens of thousands of Soviet Jews would follow the same path: Vienna, Italy, America.

Of course, it wasn't that simple with Mom, Dad, and Rubin traveling by car from Kaunas to Brest, on the border of Poland, and then by train to Warsaw and yet another train to Vienna. I'm often asked why Uncle Vlad chose Minnesota of all places to live in America. According to my father, Vlad once saw the city of Minneapolis on the cover of *Amerika*, a Soviet propaganda magazine. During an entrance interview in Italy, he was asked by an American official where he would like to live in America. Vlad remembered that magazine cover and simply said Minneapolis. Little did he know that a Siberian climate awaited him in the great state of Minnesota! I also remember asking Vlad the same question, and I could have sworn he said that he that he preferred to live in Boston or Los Angeles but that the American government wanted to distribute the Soviet Jewish population more evenly across the fruited plain. Either way, he ended up in Minnesota, and so did we. In a twist of fate, after living in America for about forty years, Vlad and Tanya moved to Israel to be closer to their younger son, who made Aliyah, along with his family.

My parents and brother arrived in Minnesota on July 11, 1975, after a nearly three-month trek through Vienna and Italy. They had $500 to their name, a host family for a few months, and some assistance from the Jewish Family Service of St. Paul. Mom was a few months pregnant with me; as I was growing up, my parents would quip that I was "Made in Italy." Just weeks after arriving in America a doctor suggested to my mom that she consider terminating the pregnancy since life was tough enough being an immigrant. Over the years I have often thought how difficult it must have been for my parents to welcome a baby into the world just as they were getting started in a new country. I am eternally grateful that they chose to give me life.

English was my father's second language and my mother's fourth. Within three months they were told to get a job since there was no public support whatsoever. They worked hard; Mom teaching piano and Dad taking whichever job he could find. Within four years they had saved enough to get a mortgage and buy a house near the Mississippi River, which they still call home today.

My dad, Dimitry, was born in 1942 in Kuybishev, Russia—a city named after a member of the politburo and today known by its pre-Communist name of Samara. My grandmother Elizaveta fled the invading Germans with most of Moscow, returning when the Germans were rebutted. My dad still remembers crying the day Stalin died on March 5, 1953; when I was growing up, he would always add that Prokofiev had the misfortune of dying on the same day. How could he not cry with the rest of the Soviet Union? It was Uncle Joe who had saved the Motherland and helped to rid the world of Hitler. I write this with more than a fair amount of sarcasm given Stalin's butchery and the realpolitik necessity that forced the world to accept the Soviets as part of the world order or face Nazi Armageddon. Of course, the world was trading one Armageddon for another. My father's perspective on Stalin swiftly evolved with the rest of the Soviet Union and about twenty years later he would leave for a better life in America. My dad's politics shaped me in innumerable ways, not least of which was an emphatic anti-Communism that defined my childhood. His foresight about Russia's inherent inability to become a democracy or long-term friend to the West is one of the clearest memories I have when he reacted to the death of the Soviet Union in 1991. I asked him if Russia would become a democracy and he simply said, "Maybe in fifty years." His instincts were more accurate than those of most of the State Department's policy experts.

My mom Celia was born in Vilnius, Lithuania, in 1947. This postwar birth was typical of the global baby boom, but these weren't happy times. I sometimes think about how it took the death of someone to result in someone else's birth. That was the case with my mom's side of the family. To illustrate this point, take my grandfather Michael: He came back from the front in 1945, where he served in the Red Army, to find that his wife and young son had been killed by the Nazis in the Kaunas ghetto. He married my grandmother Rachel in 1946 and their first child was my mom followed by her sister Svetlana eight years later. They grew up in Soviet-occupied Lithuania where 90 percent of the Jewish population had been murdered by both the Germans and their Lithuanian collaborators. Now the anti-Semitic Soviet machine that swallowed Lithuania made life difficult from both the Russian and Lithuanian sides. Mom grew up in this environment studying piano and accordion, and, as she likes to say, "speaking Yiddish at home, Russian at school, and Lithuanian on the street."

My parents ripped our family's roots out of soil that stretched back centuries in what was known as the Pale of Settlement created by Catherine the Great in 1791. This was the region beyond which Jews were not allowed. Little genealogical work has been done on our family but it's nearly certain that our roots were modest and not illustrious. No one was looking for fame or fortune back then, nor could they. Jews were living their lives in their communities and from time to time endured pogroms until one day the Nazis, an evil that could never have been imagined, came along and methodically butchered them. For those who survived, the Soviet evil took over. Reagan was criticized for calling the Soviet Union the "Evil Empire" but he was right, and we continue to see that truth today. Russia cannot help but succumb to an evil that seems to permeate its core. Russian culture is another matter, and the debate rages about culture and how it reflects the soul of the people of a nation. Germany produced Beethoven and Hitler. Italy produced Verdi and Mussolini. Russia produced Tchaikovsky and Stalin and the current leadership. Nevertheless, things do ebb and flow, with Germany and Italy once again part of the civilized world. We can remain hopeful that Russia will join them one day but the road looks long, very long.

My parents risked everything to come to America so we could plant our roots firmly in the soil of this nation. Yet as I look to the future, I become more wary of the soil in which our roots are growing. The character of our nation has changed and become more cynical, more rage filled. The happy warrior has given way to a winner-takes-all attitude in every area of life. This isn't to say that there has been no cynicism or rage in the nearly 250 years of American life. There are many dark spots, but the focus on the dark over the countless bright spots is something that has begun to strip away the red, white, and blue on which our nation was built. That equilibrium seems to have broken, with a common goal as a people disappearing. Virtues of which the American character is comprised seem to be disappearing.

My parents started anew and charted a course for our family by leaving the Soviet Union in 1975. They were followed by their parents on both sides of the family, as well as their siblings, including my father's sister Angela and mom's sister Svetlana and my cousin Jeff.

I have countless memories from my childhood house a few blocks from the Mississippi River, and one in particular from the 1980s remains emblazoned in my mind's eye: An image of a cheery-eyed man on the television in our living room, leaning back and smiling, red pen in his hand and a clipboard on his knee. The music of Bach is bellowing forth. It's *Firing Line* and my parents are watching. William F. Buckley, Jr., has entered my life.

Chapter 5

GROWING UP REAGAN IN
MONDALE'S MINNESOTA

George Will: Let me invite you to take credit for
winning the Cold War. The argument goes like this:
Without Bill Buckley, no *National Review.* Without
National Review, no Goldwater nomination. With-
out the Goldwater nomination, no conservative
takeover of the Republican Party. Without that, no
Reagan. Without Reagan, no victory in the Cold
War. Therefore, Bill Buckley won the Cold War.

William F. Buckley Jr.: That's a very nice abbrevia-
tion, and I hope you will remind historians of it.

—ABC News, October 9, 2005

t's 1984 and Ronald Reagan is up for re-election. My dad
was a Reaganite through and through. There was no doubt
in his mind that Reagan had to win, and this conviction
resonated with me at age eight. It just all made sense in the battle of "good vs. evil," "anti-Communist vs. Communist," and

"American values vs. Soviet values." One of my clearest memories from this period was in third grade at Webster Magnet School, my public school in St. Paul. It was Election Day and our teacher told us we would vote by putting our heads on our desks, closing our eyes, and raising our hands when we heard the name of the candidate we supported. I did as I was told and put my head down on my desk and closed my eyes. First, she said, "Mondale." I sat motionless. Then she said, "Reagan." I lifted my right hand up high. She then said we could open our eyes and sit back up. It turned out I was the only one in the class of approximately thirty to raise my hand for Reagan. However, unlike me, most of my classmates lifted their heads after "voting" and when I lifted mine, I noticed quite a few of them staring at me as though I had betrayed the state of Minnesota. The reason: Walter Mondale was the native son. Most of my classmates' parents were probably influencing them in a manner similar to how my dad swayed me. I stood firm and got my revenge the next day after Reagan had secured his second term in a historic landslide. Minnesota was the lone state that Mondale won.

I believe my admiration for Reagan was genuine, but would it have been the same had my parents not been from the Soviet Union? Would we have supported the native son out of loyalty? I was the only son of Russian immigrants in my class, which made me a bit of a political and cultural loner. My family believed so firmly that Reagan was the savior of the West that Rubin had a map in his room with the Soviet Union labeled "Evil Empire." We knew what we feared and weren't afraid to stand firmly against it. Then again, this was third grade and not college, and Webster Magnet School was a melting pot of cultures, races, ethnicities, and religions. It was seen as a leader in offering children of varying backgrounds an exceptional education. Most students were from middle-class families or lower-income homes in the surrounding neighborhoods. I remember the diversity of this elementary school where black, Asian, Jewish, Catholic, Lutheran, and white classmates, among many others, were friends and generally got along very well.

My warmest memories of any kind of educational experience are from these years. In 1984, we as a society and culture were just sixteen years removed from the assassination of Martin Luther King, Jr. Webster Magnet School was a product of the school integration movement. I was bused from the predominantly white neighborhood of Highland Park to Webster, which was located in a black neighborhood. Although met with mixed success nationally, busing seemed to work well in this case since Webster had an excellent reputation and offered a curriculum where children could choose electives beginning in third grade. I chose computer class and French; I credit the former with teaching me to type at a very young age, while my French never truly materialized. The fact that we were only sixteen years removed from King's assassination speaks volumes to me today when we're already more years removed from September 11, 2001. Minnesota was long known as a bastion of liberal politicians, from Hubert H. Humphrey, Jr. (LBJ's vice president) to Senator Eugene McCarthy (who toppled LBJ by challenging the sitting president in the New Hampshire primary in 1968). Nevertheless, Minnesota, like many places in the US, took time to integrate certain areas of society, and this included public schools.

Although I'm fundamentally for children attending school in the neighborhood where they reside, being bused to Webster shaped me in a way that gave me a different perspective.

My fifth- and sixth-grade teachers were both black; Ms. Stroud and Mr. Helm, respectively. They were the most formative and important teachers I had in my early life. Ms. Stroud had a banner across the top of her room that read, "A Mind Is a Terrible Thing to Waste." Little did I know at that time that this was the tagline for the United Negro College Fund. I was a good reader in fifth grade and was in the second-highest reading group. I could have been better and recall this being a concern for my parents, and during a parent-teacher conference Ms. Stroud pointed out that I had potential and should focus on improving. There was no sugar-coating it back then. She was direct and it stung because she was right. I worked on it and improved each week. She believed in me, and it paid off—with my reading improving markedly.

The following year I was placed in Mr. Helm's class, which was a coveted classroom. He was known for being the most fun and creative teacher in the school; during Thanksgiving he would serve his class a roasted turkey with all the fixings. He was someone who instilled self-confidence in each of his students. I look back at him as a Falstaff-sized figure with Cheshire cat features. My early entrepreneurial sparks came alive in his class because he was open to every idea. Some friends of mine and I wanted to start a class newspaper. He encouraged us and we did it. I suggested to him that we have a classroom president and an election to choose one. He immediately agreed. Campaigns were launched, posters designed, and elections took place every few months. As initiator, I thought I was a shoo-in for the presidency but I learned about democracy very quickly when I lost the first election. And the second. I was devastated by these losses, but Mr. Helm continued to encourage me until the third time was the charm. My mom helped me to make a "Larry for

President" T-shirt at a local shop and my campaigning became more rigorous.

Through high school I would return to Webster every year or two to visit Ms. Stroud and Mr. Helm. Ms. Stroud would go on to be named Minnesota's teacher of the year. The first teacher from St. Paul and first black teacher in the state to be so honored. The last time I saw them was when they attended my college graduation party in 1998 hosted by my parents at our house. As Mr. Helm entered with his ever-present grin, he said, "Hello, Mr. President," something he had done each and every time I visited him after sixth grade. Their belief in me still rings within me as I aim to achieve things in life. I'm eternally grateful to these teachers because they forged the foundation that would lead to dreams beyond my imagination.

If my father influenced my political outlook, it was my mother who shaped me musically and passed along the talent. She was a concert accordionist in Lithuania and taught both that instrument and piano in Lithuania and later in Moscow after my parents were wed. My grandfather played amateur harmonica but was a natural performer whom I can still see playing and finishing with a flourish, his hands in the air awaiting applause. In Minnesota, Mom quickly established her own studio after working for a friend and learning that he was taking 50 percent of her fee. This was a quick lesson in economics and finance as she realized that an entrepreneur could make more by taking on some risk. As my longtime friend, the homebuilding titan Brian Beazer, likes to say, "You have to have some skin in the game." By the time my parents bought their house—the same one where they live today—my mom had upwards of forty piano students taking weekly lessons in our basement. My father worked the night shift at a Graco factory, so in retrospect the schedule in our house was unorthodox with my parents' ships passing in the night as Mom finished with her students and Dad started to prepare to leave for work around 10:00 p.m. It's extraordinary now looking back at the sacrifices they both made for my brother and me and how in some ways we took it for granted. We knew they worked hard but we were children. I don't remember them ever complaining because they must have felt blessed to have the opportunities this country offered to those willing to work hard. Beyond these jobs they also managed, and were caretakers of, three apartment buildings about a mile from our house where my grandparents (Mom's parents to whom I referred earlier) and Dad's sister lived upon arriving in America in 1980. My brother would paint apartments with Mom, and Dad would repair anything that broke from electrical sockets to faucets. There were nearly sixty units to oversee and my parents did all this with a full-fledged commitment reporting directly to the buildings' owners.

My mom was, and is, a very direct person, so when she felt that the family needed to earn more money, she literally walked into one of these apartment buildings and knocked on the door of the caretaker after seeing a "Help Wanted" sign. Her English was still choppy after only a few years in America but she so impressed the man who opened the door that the job went to my parents. The man who answered, Drew Bjorklund, along with his wife Claire, became among our family's closest friends and we would spend holidays together throughout the 1980s.

That was the magnetic connection my parents were able to make with people. I'm not detracting anything from my dad but my mom's talent and trait as a performer, something she gave up completely soon after arriving in St. Paul, came through in other ways. The performer might have left the stage but the whole world remained a stage for her in the way she interacted with students and everyone around her. Performers have to be fearless since they put themselves on display before an audience each time they step onstage. My mom passed this fearlessness along to me and instilled a self-confidence in me that I don't think I otherwise would possess.

In my early teens I became more and more interested in politicians and business leaders. Although I wanted to be a concert pianist, I was also fascinated by powerful figures, both living and historic. I recall clearly telling my mom that I wanted to meet the CEO of a company in Minnesota. Her reply to me was simple: "Write him a letter." Mom's encouragement also led me to realize my dreams of meeting my classical music heroes backstage at concert halls and asking for autographs. These included John Browning, Radu Lupu, Itzhak Perlman, and André Watts. She later told me that even if she would never do these things herself, she saw that I was interested and eager and decided to encourage and nurture my interests. There's a wall of fame in my parents' house lined with autographs from dozens of artists who graced the stages of Minnesota and eventually New York. Some of these artists would become my clients.

There was never a reaction from my mom that discouraged me from trying something and pursuing it. She would reference a Russian adage having to do with going to the top person, "Go to the head, not the ass." My dad was always supportive. This made for a very powerful blend, which instilled in me the belief that I could actually meet anyone. It would serve me very well.

So began my letter writing in the 1990s to CEOs, senior executives, senators, classical music artists and leaders, celebrities, and people from all walks of life. My collection from that era includes responses from personalities as varying as investment banker Herbert Allen; advertising legend David Bell, president and CEO of Bozell Worldwide; media executive Tom Rogers; Minnesota Senator Rudy Boschwitz; Steinway & Sons executive Peter Goodrich; and Isaac Stern, legendary concert violinist and the man who was responsible for saving Carnegie Hall from the wrecking ball.

All of these experiences shaped me and prepared me to write the letter that would change my life.

Chapter 6

HAPPY DAYS ON THE UPPER WEST SIDE

Sitting in my room, having just moved to New York in 1994, with barely a friend, I took solace in reading the most recent collection of columns by William F. Buckley, Jr. The cover of *Happy Days Were Here Again: Reflections of a Libertarian Journalist* had a quintessential photograph of Bill leaning back in his chair, index finger over his pursed lips, and his red pen at the ready. This was much like the earliest image I had of Bill on television in our living room. Every so often Bill would compile his columns from a decade or an epoch and publish them in book form. This book's title was a play on FDR's 1932 campaign slogan "Happy Days Are Here Again" and resonated with my grief over not having been accepted to the Juilliard School, while Bill was reminiscing about the Reagan era, which was supplanted by the Clinton years.

Several columns in the book were dedicated to classical music, including one where Bill interviewed himself for *The New York Times* in advance of playing a Bach concerto with the Phoenix

Symphony. It was titled "An Attempt at Explaining" and published on October 1, 1989. Bill recounts that the Phoenix Symphony invited him to play any Bach keyboard concerto on two years' notice. Given his busy schedule, he asked his friend the harpsichordist Fernando Valenti to identify the shortest Bach concerto: "The F minor takes only eight and one-half minutes." With this information Bill devised a plan of attack. He explained in the interview:

> Eight and one-half minutes! I was being given, potentially, twenty-eight months to discipline my fingers to play eight and one-half minutes, which comes down to about three and a half months per minute, or about one week per note. Figuring it out that way, I could perform the "Flight of the Bumblebee" in a couple of years!

William F. Buckley, Jr. performing Bach on harpsichord with the Phoenix Symphony in 1989. Courtesy of Christopher Buckley.

I cracked up while reading and thought Bill had to be joking. It's impossible to learn a piece of music this way. The interview continued in the same vein, with him discussing his "practice" strategy with various teachers and friends, including the foremost Bach interpreter of that time: Rosalyn Tureck. Nearly everyone tells Bill that—with his countless commitments and Energizer Bunny schedule—it would be nearly impossible for him to learn the concerto and play it at all, let alone at concert level, unless he gave up everything and practiced three hours a day. Well, Bill, who was raised in a house with five pianos and a mandatory forty-five-minute daily practice session, and who dreamt of becoming a pianist until his early teens, proved everyone wrong. Not only did he learn the concerto but he proposed a performance date to Phoenix in thirteen months as opposed to the two-year offer. He decided that dedicating two years to the project would just be too much.

As I read page after page it dawned on me: "Here I am in New York and William F. Buckley, Jr. lives in New York. He loves the harpsichord, piano, classical music, and Bach. He is my hero: an anti-Communist warrior, a fighter against anti-Semitism, defender of freedom, a Renaissance man, and the man credited with making Reagan a reality. If not for this man and his philosophy, my family and people like us, would never have made it to America." I saw that direct line from Bill to my very existence in America. That's when I decided I would write a letter to him! In fact, it would be a "thank you" letter and as my "thank you" I would offer him the gift of music: a private recital. This would be my thanks to him for everything he had done for us.

How did I get to the Upper West Side? Music has been part of my life since the first days of my life: From Mom's impromptu accordion concerts at home to the piano lessons in our house; orchestra and opera recordings playing day and night; and Dad's Saturday morning tradition of waking us up with the music of Vladimir Vysotsky, the Russian Bob Dylan, blaring in the living room. We had two upright pianos, one white Yamaha in our living room, and a Baldwin in Mom's basement piano studio. I gravitated to the piano naturally but wasn't a prodigy. There's a picture of me at about a year old where I'm on my tiptoes holding onto the side of the Yamaha while Mom watches Rubin play the piano. My talent became apparent in a few ways, including singing melodies from random sections of a symphony, which so impressed a family friend that he mentioned it to my mom. My playing was that of a very talented grade school kid playing Clementi sonatinas and some Mozart. It's common knowledge that parents should never teach their children to play an instrument or drive a car. Teaching Rubin and me piano was left to our family friend Shelly Singer, with whom my mom shared the piano studio before striking out on her own. Rubin quit playing when he was about twelve years old. I outgrew Shelly after a few years and at age ten Mom took me to Yakov Gelfand, a teacher who lived about a mile from our house.

What prompted the change in teachers was my insistence on learning Scott Joplin's "The Entertainer." I refused to learn an easy version and wanted to play the original. For one of my birthdays, my parents gave me a Scott Joplin compendium with all of his best-known Ragtime pieces. I set out to learn "The Entertainer" and conquered it on my own. My persistence made Mom realize there might be something there in terms of talent. "The Entertainer" became my showpiece, and I played it for everyone everywhere, including at school assemblies, an event at the Jewish Community Center, and, of course, family gatherings, where I became the star. This, along with some classical works, made me think I was very good at the piano, especially with all the compliments I was receiving.

All of this changed when I arrived at Yakov's house. There I received mostly criticism and only a back-handed compliment, if that. After our first lesson he looked at my mom and said, "You should have brought him to me when he was seven." This became a running theme for years to come. He commented on my flat fingers, sloppy technique, and inconsistent rhythm. The one positive thing he saw was "potential."

Yakov Gelfand was born in 1932 in Leningrad. His mother Chaya was an extremely gifted pianist and pedagogue. A contemporary of Sergei Prokofiev's, she placed second to him in a piano concerto competition, I was told. Yakov's family survived the Siege of Leningrad by boiling the flour off of wallpaper in order to find some sustenance in those very dark days. He would go on to graduate from the Leningrad Conservatory and became a professor there. Much like my parents, he and his other Jewish colleagues would leave the Soviet Union when the gates opened in the 1970s and start life anew in the West.

Over time I would realize that it was my incredible luck that Yakov ended up part of the Soviet Jewish diaspora in St. Paul. He was horrible at self-promotion and thus wasn't the most famous piano professor in the Twin Cities, but he was the best. He had a reputation as someone who could take a child that showed signs of talent and shape him or her into a real musician. He would invite his mother to sit in on my lessons from time to time. She cut a diminutive figure and was all the more intimidating. She seemed to wear a perpetual scowl on her face during these sessions. She not only survived World War II, but also being hit by a bus in her eighties. She was formidable.

It was almost a form of "bad cop, bad cop" to have these two Russian pedagogues in the room with me and it was devised to exert maximal pressure on the students. Many years later, I found out that she was quite fond of my playing and was there to build my confidence, not to frighten me. One year in Salzburg I visited Grigory Solokov, considered by the music world to be among the greatest pianists, and conveyed greetings from Yakov. I learned from Yakov that he and his mother were Sokolov's first teachers.

Yakov was the kind of teacher who would fill up a page with tiny scribbles and comments in red pencil. It was a veritable sea of notes. J.S. Bach's Prelude and Fugue in B-Flat minor from Book I of the Well-Tempered Clavier is a prime example—there were almost as many comments from Yakov as musical notes from Bach. That said, it did the trick, and Yakov's notes became the directions of an expert driver on a roadmap. He knew exactly where he was going and leading his pupils.

Yakov would often say that three elements are necessary to become a performer: technique, musicianship, and artistry. If you think about it, there isn't a truly great performer who doesn't embody all three of these. I added a fourth element, which I believe I lacked: capacity. You can have the three elements of which Yakov spoke, but without capacity you can't survive the grueling labor required of any true performer. You need the capacity to learn countless scores and give concerts every few days at the highest quality. There are even examples of those who do have capacity and all other elements and still can't sustain a major career. To achieve success as a performer is somewhat of a mystery after all is said and done.

Yakov didn't suffer fools when it came to musicians. He called most pianists "idiots" because of what he considered their boundless disregard for the score. This may be extreme but he had a point, especially when it came to recorded music influencing a young pianist's studies. I went through a Vladimir Horowitz stage where I couldn't get enough of his recordings and mimicked him without even knowing it. Yakov, not so subtly, told me to stop listening to recordings of music I was learning and to focus on the score. I thought he didn't want the romantic side of me to flourish as a young performer and was imposing his structure on me. We had shouting matches over disagreements on this point. However, I began to understand that if he didn't reel in my expressiveness, the concert stage would derail me completely. Without structure there would be chaos. He was right.

I'll never forget that when I would complain about a piano on which I was to perform, Yakov would say in Russian that "balls get in the way of a bad dancer." My mom, who attended some of my lessons, was horrified by these jokes and adages directed at a teenager. But Yakov had a point and indeed the fault was the pianist's and not the piano's no matter how inadequate the piano seemed. I would never complain about pianos going forward and had to find a way to adapt my technique to whatever limitations an instrument might have had.

Yakov's approach to teaching was fascinating in that he was reluctant to assign the most popular pieces to his students. He had me learn Beethoven's Piano Sonata Op. 90 for my conservatory auditions instead of warhorses like the *Waldstein* or *Appassionata*. This grated on me until I understood that this was to differentiate me and have me stand out to the jury since almost no one would consider Op. 90 for an audition. The same went for much of my teenage repertoire, which included Brahms's *Variations and Fugue on a Theme by Handel*, Chopin's

F-Sharp minor polonaise, Debussy's *L'isle joyeuse*, Liszt's Transcendental Etude No. 12 *Chasse-neige*, Bach's E minor partita, and Liszt's *Rigoletto Paraphrase*, which became my calling card. In retrospect the many pieces I studied with Yakov were part of his grand strategy to make me a complete pianist capable of tackling any piece of music. He never assigned scales and arpeggios. Instead, he would use those patterns within the works themselves to shape and reshape my technique. I arrived with flat fingers and uneven pianist touch and left with a natural pianistic technique where I never complained of pain in my shoulders or forearms unlike many colleagues. So much of pianism can be forced and uncomfortable, but with Yakov the aim was to move as little as possible. If ever there was anti-flair, it was Yakov. He recognized the greatness of the composers to which we, in the "business" of music, owe our thanks and our livelihood. Sometimes we are so absorbed by the moment, we forget that we are able to make a living playing music because there were those who dedicated themselves selflessly to composing and instructing, not expecting to be royally compensated. The pedagogue is the ultimate example of the keeper of the flame for the composer. This was Yakov. He kept the flame alive and made my full potential come to light.

* * *

During my teens I practiced between three to five hours a day. The piano was the center of my life. I thought that the concert stage would be my future and dreamt of a major career. However, there was always a doubt in my mind. Although I played extremely well, I wasn't wowing audiences around the world, or even outside the city of St. Paul. That's not to say that every concert pianist is a prodigy or early bloomer, but I knew that I didn't have the level of talent that drives the confidence one has to have for a life on the stage. Even if I had had everything, there is never a guarantee of a career. For every pianist or musician with a career there are hundreds of very talented people with mid-level to low-level careers. This isn't to say these people aren't happy. For many people doing what they love is all that matters, so spending hours practicing, teaching, and cobbling gigs and performances into a career is worth it for them.

During my two summers at the Aspen Music Festival & School in 1993 and 1994, I encountered people from around the world whose immense talent and capacity for learning music were far beyond mine. Self-doubt about a professional career was taking shape but I still wanted to give a career a go, and I wanted to move to New York. Instead of college I applied and auditioned to several conservatories, including the Curtis Institute of Music, The Juilliard School, and the Manhattan School of Music. Curtis was a very far reach generally reserved for prodigies; Juilliard was all that really mattered to me. The Manhattan School of Music, located in Juilliard's former building near Columbia University, was my safety school.

The admissions letters came back one by one. Curtis rejected me. Juilliard waitlisted me. The Manhattan School of Music accepted me into the studio of Yakov's friend Arkady Aronov.

I had a contact on the Juilliard faculty, the great American pianist John Browning, for whom I had played when I was thirteen. He wrote back that he was absent from the jury the day of my audition but "I hope you get in and that all goes well in your future." Soon after, Juilliard updated me that no one was accepted from the waiting list.

I couldn't believe it. My dream was shattered.

Nonetheless, I decided on the Manhattan School of Music and my parents agreed to support my decision knowing how much I wanted to be in New York. It was going to be very expensive for them but they would find a way. None of us was thinking about the future rationally. In retrospect these were decisions based on dreams. Some can criticize the decision to pursue a career in music when I already had doubts about where the road would lead. Then again, this was exactly what my parents did when they left the Soviet Union. They didn't know where the road would lead. My parents said they would give me a chance in New York and I would have to prove myself. They flew to New York with me in August 1994 for orientation and helped me to move into my apartment: a single room, one hundred square feet, in a four-bedroom apartment on the corner of West 81st and Broadway for $500 a month. This was nearly what their mortgage was then. The location was prime Upper West Side—on the same block as Jerry Seinfeld's fictional apartment—and the proximity to Zabar's became an obsession for me with orders from my parents to bring back smoked salmon on trips home.

This was Giuliani's New York and the city was on the rebound from decades of crime. Still, my parents were nervous about safety and the room was tiny. I was able to use the apartment's living room and practice on the landlord's shabby piano from time to time. One bathroom was shared by three of the roommates. None of this mattered to me. I had made it to New York!

My parents flew back to St. Paul and Mom was distraught after leaving me all alone in New York. I was on my own, but my parents gave me the tools to survive.

* * *

I began to think about what I would write to William F. Buckley, Jr. The focus was intense and my goal was very clear: I had to meet this great man.

Chapter 7

THE GOLDEN TICKET

*Thank you for your warm letter which
so nicely expresses your ambition.*

—WILLIAM F. BUCKLEY, JR., RESPONSE
LETTER TO ME, OCTOBER 17, 1994

n 1994, I didn't yet have a computer, and my handwriting
was terrible. I borrowed a word processor from Dina Ganz,
a family friend living in New York, so I could type a letter
to Bill. I never made a copy of that letter before sending it. The
Yale Library, which houses the Buckley Archive, couldn't find it.
What I can recall from my letter was that I expressed my ambition to become a pianist and mentioned that I had enrolled at
the Manhattan School of Music after not being accepted at Juilliard. I continued by expressing my desire to meet him so that
I could give him a thank you present in the form of a private
recital. I wanted to "thank you in person for having embold-
ened Soviet Jews to come to America and make it here." That
last sentence was emblazoned in my memory. I found *National
Review*'s address (back then it was 150 East 35th Street, New

York, New York, 10016) and sent the letter via FedEx. It was near the end of September 1994.

I've grown more patient over the years but patience isn't part of my DNA. At age eighteen I was much less patient and wanted instant responses. This was 1994, pre-internet days. After a few days I wanted to be sure that Bill had received my letter, so, naturally, what would one do but call Bill's assistant? I dialed the number for *National Review* and a receptionist answered.

> NR receptionist: National Review.

> Me: Hello, may I speak with Mr. Buckley's assistant?

> NR receptionist: Who may I say is calling?

> Me: Lawrence Perelman.

> NR receptionist: Please hold.

> Bill's assistant: Hello? [English accent.]

> Me: Hello, is this Mr. Buckley's assistant?

> Bill's assistant: Yes. How may I help you?

> Me: My name is Lawrence Perelman and I wanted to make sure that Mr. Buckley received a letter I sent.

> Bill's assistant: How would I know—he receives hundreds of letters every week.

> Me: But I'm the eighteen-year-old pianist who wrote to him—

Bill's assistant: Ah, yes, we did receive it and he'll reply in due course. [Hangs up.]

She simply hung up! Nevertheless, it was confirmed. They had my letter and "he would reply in due course," which was an expression I had never heard before, but it made sense that Bill's office would speak in that manner. I would later learn that the voice on the other end of the line was Frances Bronson, Bill's longtime assistant.

This only added fuel to the fire of my impatience. "Due course?" When would that be? When would I hear from him? Days went by. A week. I was practicing piano and going to class but always front of mind was "due course, due course, due course." When would he write back to me? Then I would think about the contents of the letter and that it would most likely be a form letter or rejection of some kind. I analyzed all angles.

I recounted everything to my parents on the phone. They were always excited participants and lived vicariously through the stories I told them about New York and my early adventures. They were always by my side even though they were over a thousand miles away.

Each day any mail for me would be left on the floor near the bedroom door. I would walk towards the door expecting to find an envelope. It was nearly two weeks since I'd sent the letter, and nothing. Then one day I turned the corner, walked down the hallway, and, there, on the floor was a white standard-size envelope. The paper stock felt elegant and the name on the upper-left-hand corner in light blue italics was *William F. Buckley, Jr.* I couldn't believe it. My heart began to race. I ran into my room and used a letter opener so as not to rip the envelope. The first thought that crossed my mind was that this would be a form letter. I'd received those before from those to whom I had written. I settled down and opened the letter and started to read:

October 17, 1994

Dear Mr. Perelman:

Thank you for your warm letter which so nicely expresses your ambition. I have been ill and for that reason am terribly behind on any number of commitments. But I hope to have the opportunity when I come back from Europe early next March to meet with you and have the pleasure of hearing you play.

Yours cordially,
Wm. F. Buckley, Jr.

I felt like Charlie Bucket to Buckley's Willy Wonka. This was my golden ticket! William F. Buckley, Jr., had accepted my offer to play him a private "thank you" recital. I was dumbstruck and called my parents. They were thrilled and amazed. I couldn't stop talking or thinking about it. He took the time to write back, signed the letter in his trademark red ink, and actually invited me to play for him! Wow, what a person!

The waiting began again, but this time there was a goal in sight. I knew that come March 1995, I would call his office and arrange the date. March couldn't come quickly enough and when March 1 arrived, I called Frances Bronson at *National Review*. This time she didn't put the phone down abruptly but proposed meeting Bill on April 24, 1995, at 5:00 p.m. at 73 East 73rd Street. I immediately accepted. I was briefly disappointed that I would have to wait until April but reminded myself that this was actually happening. I wanted to emulate Bill's style so I wrote a letter to him confirming the date and sending along a program from a recital I had recently given:

Mr. William F. Buckley, Jr.
National Review
150 East 35th Street
New York, New York 10016

Dear Mr. Buckley:

Thank you for agreeing to hear me play on the 24th of April, 1995. I am looking forward to our meeting with great excitement.

A program, from a recent recital, is enclosed for your interest.

Once again, thank you for your time, and I look forward to meeting you in person on the 24th.

Yours cordially,
Lawrence Gabriel Perelman

It's fun to read that I closed the letter with "Yours cordially," the way he closed his letter to me. I was so proud of mimicking him, and Bill not only made my day back in 1994 but my year in 1995. I was excited. This gave me so much confidence and I hadn't even met him. Happy days were indeed here again—for me and for Bill. The Republicans swept both houses of Congress in November 1994, which led to a resurgence in interest in publications like *National Review*. Years later Bill would often mention that 1994 was the only profitable year for *National Review*.

Alongside the excitement of the impending meeting with Bill was the tragedy of the Oklahoma City bombing on April 19, 1995. That horrific event made me think about whether our meeting would proceed. Bill was a very high-profile person— would he allow a complete stranger into his home? Would he require a background check for me? After all, Bill was a former CIA operative. These were thoughts crossing my mind as each day passed and April 24 came into view.

Gene Tupper, my contact at Steinway Hall on 57th Street, kindly arranged for me to practice in the "Rachmaninoff Room," which had a beautiful piano and a painting of the great pianist and composer. This room was made available to concert artists visiting New York who needed a practice room. When that room wasn't available Gene allowed me to practice in a showroom as long as customers weren't around. This was generally frowned upon by Steinway Hall staff but Gene held the keys to the castle.

* * *

It's important to elaborate on Steinway Hall, which was central to my existence in New York for two decades when the flagship showroom was unceremoniously sold and moved to a non-descript location. My first visit to Steinway Hall coincided with my first trip to New York with a group from my synagogue in 1991. We had a strict itinerary of synagogue and deli visits, along with the usual sightseeing, including the World Trade Center, Statue of Liberty, and Ellis Island. I made a point to tell the chaperons that I had to visit Steinway Hall on 57th Street. This was the main reason I went on the trip. The chaperons were reluctant to take me there, but I lobbied one of them incessantly, who finally agreed. I was a persuasive fifteen-year-old. Prior to the trip I had done my homework, having spoken with a piano sales representative I knew in Minneapolis who had an important contact at Steinway Hall. She put in a word with Gene Tupper, originally from Minnesota, who turned out to be Steinway's most important sales executive in New York, which meant the most important one in the country. Gene was a World War II veteran and someone I would get to know very well in the years ahead. He served on Iwo Jima and one day showed me photographs of his time on the island. He kept these personal World War II photographs in the drawer of his desk. I never asked him why he kept the photos there but I think it might have been to remind him how fortunate he was compared to the soldiers who didn't make it home.

Gene's desk was located in the prime position at the entrance of Steinway Hall under a heroic painting portraying a great composer in the style of Delacroix. Gene was always immaculately dressed in suit and tie with perfectly coiffed red hair and glasses. This was a man who was tailored to sell what today would be a $100,000 piano to a corporate titan or give a warm welcome to a great artist. He was all class.

I walked into gilded Steinway Hall that first time and felt as though I belonged. This building dated to 1927 and had hosted every major pianist since then. This is where everyone from Rachmaninoff to Horowitz, Rubinstein to Argerich would select their pianos in the gritty basement for New York performances and beyond. Carnegie Hall is just half a block away. This was a pianist's Holy Land where the basement and a room on the second floor held dozens of nearly nine-foot-long Model D concert grand pianos, most built in the factory in Queens and several built in the Hamburg factory. The echo of the showroom's domed ceiling created a surreal acoustical effect when one touched the keys of the piano situated within it. Gene welcomed me like a member of the family and I passed along greetings from his friend in Minnesota. We spoke for a bit and then he invited me to play on a piano. He gave me a book on the history of Steinway as a gift. Soon the chaperon and I were back on 57th Street and a few days later I was back home in Minnesota. This experience was seared in my mind and I just knew I would be back.

* * *

As I created my program for the recital, I knew Bill would expect Bach. I chose the C-Sharp minor Prelude and Fugue from Book I of the Well-Tempered Clavier. I was preparing my end-of-year program for the Manhattan School so I drew from that as well, also choosing Debussy's *L'isle joyeuse* and Liszt's tremendously difficult Transcendental Etude No. 12, *Chasse-neige*, a flurry of notes meant to evoke a snowstorm.

I wasn't sure what to bring Bill and couldn't arrive empty handed; Russian tradition required a guest to bring something, no matter how small. What do you buy for someone who has everything? I discussed this with a friend, and since I was too young to buy alcohol, he said, "Bring him fresh squeezed orange juice. *Everyone* loves fresh squeezed orange juice." I thought about it and decided that, although seemingly odd, I would go this route.

I practiced Bach, Liszt, and Debussy at Steinway Hall and anticipated the day I would play for "Mr. Buckley."

Chapter 8

MEETING MR. BUCKLEY

You can spend an hour playing the piano and develop
your capacity to think, even to create, and certainly
to invest yourself with a feeling for priorities.

—WILLIAM F. BUCKLEY, JR.,
MILES GONE BY: A LITERARY AUTOBIOGRAPHY

The day arrived and I headed over to Zabar's to buy the fresh squeezed orange juice. I bought two pints and they fit nicely in a Zabar's paper bag. I was excited and nervous about the day; 5:00 p.m. seemed to be taking forever to arrive. I took a bus across to 79th Street and Madison then walked down to 73rd Street and Madison. This was the Upper East Side, the heart of opulence and wealth. I had never been in a historic apartment building and didn't know what to expect from Bill's apartment. I was about fifteen minutes early so I walked around the block to find the building. What kind of building would it be? A brownstone? A doorman building? I had no idea. I looked for the street address and nearly came to the corner of 73rd and Park Avenue when I saw the number

"73" above a doorway. This must be it. There stood two intricately decorated iron doors. It was not yet 5:00 p.m. so I went around the corner to Park Avenue and back again until 4:59 p.m. I realized that this was a private entrance to his home in this enormous building on the corner of East 73rd Street and Park Avenue. I would later learn that the building was 778 Park Avenue and considered one of the most exclusive buildings in all of Manhattan and also home to Brooke Astor. The previous owner of the Buckley residence was Dag Hammarskjöld, the second UN Secretary-General who died in a plane crash in 1961.

I rang the doorbell at 5:00 p.m. and within seconds the door opened and there stood William F. Buckley, Jr. Our exchange remains vivid in my mind.

"Hello," said Bill.

"Mr. Buckley. It's an honor to meet you. I'm Larry Perelman."

"Hi Larry. Please come in."

"Thank you, Mr. Buckley. I brought you something: Fresh squeezed orange juice."

Bill quipped in his trademark drawn out accent, "From Is-ra-el?"

I took Bill literally and replied, "No, it's from Zabar's!"

It was a hilarious start to our first meeting.

We walked inside and into a world I had only seen in movies or pictures in design magazines like my mom's collection of *Architectural Digest* as she embarked on a second career as an interior decorator. There was a harpsichord on the left as we walked through the entrance on the marble hallway floor which then revealed the grand staircase sweeping up to the second floor. There were paintings all over—I wondered whether these were by Bill himself, since I had read that he had taken a painting lesson from Marc Chagall—and a Victorian or Gilded Age feel to each room. Others would refer to the style as "camp," for which Mrs. Buckley, Pat, was known.

We entered the library, which one could simply describe as the Red Room since everything, from the wall coverings to the chairs and sofas, was red. There was a bar off to the side and Bill asked what I would like to drink. I asked for a Coke and we sat down for a chat. Joining Bill was someone in his mid-twenties whom I later learned was Drew Oliver, the son of an old family friend of Bill's. We chatted for ten minutes or so with Bill asking various questions about my life, my parents leaving the Soviet Union, and about the music I was going to play. I distinctly recall bringing along a copy of Dostoyevsky's *The Brothers Karamazov*. I was taking a Russian literature class at Columbia University and wanted to emphasize my intellectual side; this was again my aspiration and slight insecurity since I was meeting such a giant thinker. Bill saw the book and proceeded to mention something about Whittaker Chambers and *The Brothers Karamazov*. He said it so slyly that I missed it. However, in the midst of writing this book I found an article in *National Review* that stated, "[writer] John Leonard said that to lunch with Whittaker Chambers was to encounter by turns each of the Karamazov brothers." I'll never know if this is what Bill said but the fact that he mentioned Whittaker Chambers, an iconic figure of the Cold War era, already made my afternoon.

Bill put me at ease and there was no pretense at all. I expected him to be dressed formally—I wore a suit and tie—but he was very causal in khakis, collared shirt, and a *National Review* sweater. It was expectation versus reality, and the real William F. Buckley, Jr., wasn't an intimidating Yale Debate Association sparring partner. The daunting *Firing Line* host was a role he played and inhabited for the program or, as I would later learn, at dinner parties. What I saw here was an approachable and incredibly secure human being comfortable in his own skin.

We moved to the living room, which was expansive, running from what would have been the corner of Park Avenue and 73rd Street to the door that Bill opened to greet me. It looked like something out of *Downton Abbey*. There were giant windows with ornately decorated curtains, paintings lit by small lamps, and tables with dozens of little tchotchkes throughout the room. It must have been about a thousand square feet and the ceiling at least twenty feet high. There were enough couches, *chaise longues*, and various stools to seat thirty guests. Against the wall opposite the 73rd Street wall stood the main attraction: a massive Bösendorfer piano with a piano bench big enough for two and with a soft needlepoint padding. Bill took me over to the piano and began to fiddle with the piano lamps, ultimately triumphing in turning them on. I played a scale and thought to myself, "this could have used a tune." Of course, I had trained in Yakov's school of not complaining about a piano and determined that it would be up to me to make do with whatever the conditions. The piano was obviously very old but it was William F. Buckley, Jr.'s piano! I sat down and Bill and Drew took their seats.

As I began to play I realized that all of the practicing and lessons had paid off since the piano itself was tricky. But after a few minutes I was in the zone and so high from the experience of meeting Bill that the music just washed forth from me. I began with the Bach, proceeded to the Debussy, and finished off with the hyper-virtuosic Liszt Transcendental Etude, which ends like an intense blizzard fading to black. Bill and Drew applauded after each piece of music. Between each work we discussed the music and composer. I could tell that Bill was enjoying himself.

I was in awe of Bill and being in his presence. The occasion sped by as quickly as the months awaiting it had moved slowly. I could feel it drawing to a close and made sure to again thank him for everything he had done for my family as a great Cold Warrior. Fifty years separated us that day with Bill, sixty-nine, old enough to be my grandfather.

As we made our way back past the enormous spiral staircase and the harpsichord, Bill wished me luck with my studies. I thanked him and he thanked me again for the recital. It was a few minutes past 6:00 p.m. and I walked out of that Narnian door back onto East 73rd Street. I immediately asked myself, "How do I get back in?" and went back to my room on the Upper West Side to call and regale my parents with the most incredible afternoon of my life.

Chapter 9

GOODBYE, NEW YORK

The glow of visiting Bill and playing for him stayed with me for a long time. I recounted the encounter endlessly to friends and acquaintances who would listen. Bill wrote me a letter on April 27, 1995:

> Dear Larry,
>
> I was very pleased to meet you. You played beautifully, and you spoke with great maturity and wisdom. I wish you all the best, and please stay in touch.
>
> Yours cordially,
> Wm. F. Buckley, Jr.

I cherished this letter along with the first letter he sent— and took literally that he wanted to stay in touch. Who knows if he really meant it, but for me it was an invitation to keep him apprised of my activities.

I loved New York. I made many friends and couldn't get enough of the cultural offerings, from Carnegie Hall to the Metropolitan Opera to the Metropolitan Museum. Access to everything and everyone made New York the right place for a college student with an insatiable desire to meet people and feel a part of this metropolis. I practiced often at Steinway Hall and got to know many artists and every executive there, including a wonderful man named Peter Goodrich, the vice president for Concert & Artist Activities, basically Steinway's liaison to artists, many of my artistic heroes. Peter would become a great friend, giving me access to Steinway Hall after Gene Tupper's retirement. In many respects Steinway Hall became like a second home and I easily spent several days a week there. That's where I would make some lifelong friends, with an especially enduring one in the form of Daniell Revenaugh.

I was going through a Churchillian phase, which piqued my interest in cigars. The images of Churchill with a cigar were iconic and drove my fascination. I also noted that Bill smoked cigars. During a trip home to Minnesota, my parents and I visited Isaac Ganz, a family friend, who had also left the Soviet Union in the 1970s. He was showing us some photographs when he opened a desk drawer inside of which was a box of Cuban Romeo y Julieta cigars. The box of twenty cigars was sealed and more than two decades old. He said I could have it.

What to do with a box of dried out Cuban cigars? Why not sell them? I returned to New York and asked Clarie, the receptionist at Steinway Hall and basically the Hall's den mother, whom she might know with an affinity for cigars. She mentioned the pianist Daniell Revenaugh. I didn't recognize the name, and this was 1995, pre-internet search engines, so I couldn't get too much information. Claire said she would ask him to call me the next time he was in New York.

One day I got a phone call, and a gruff voice on the other end said, "I hear you've got some Cuban cigars." I confirmed that I did, and the person identified himself as Daniell Revenaugh. We set a meeting date at Steinway Hall. I was practicing in the Rachmaninoff Room when there was a knock on the door. Revenaugh, sixty-one, a somewhat burly, brusque, and disheveled man, cut an imposing and no-nonsense figure at first meeting. He was visiting from Berkeley, California, which he called home. However, he mentioned almost immediately that he had properties in Tallahassee, Florida, and in Lausanne, Switzerland. Quite the variety. The first order of business was for me to play for him. He was complimentary and then made some critiques. I quickly learned that he had been a student of the legendary pianist Egon Petri who was himself a student of Ferruccio Busoni, one of the greatest pianists in history, as well as an important, yet underappreciated, composer. Revenaugh mentioned Busoni within minutes, as well as the fact that he had the largest collection of Busoni letters in private hands. He also mentioned that he had produced and conducted the first recording of Busoni's monumental Piano Concerto in C major with John Ogdon at the piano in the late 1960s released on EMI. Now I realized that I knew Revenaugh's name from that recording and its place in music history.

Revenaugh would go on to become an important part of my life and a sounding board for many of my entrepreneurial endeavors in the music world. It was also during this time in the fall of 1995 that I was thinking of transferring from the

Manhattan School of Music and moving back to Minnesota to finish my undergraduate studies at Macalester College in St. Paul. Although I really wanted to remain in New York, it was costly for my parents, and I didn't feel that my career prospects as a pianist were realistic. I was playing seriously but my mind often focused on the business side of music and an ambition to see classical music have a greater prominence in people's lives through increased visibility in the media landscape. Revenaugh would introduce me to Martha Argerich, arguably the greatest living pianist, and was tremendously supportive when it came to providing feedback on ideas. He was known for inventions like the lower lid for the grand piano and for trying to popularize classical music with the Electric Symphony in the 1970s, an attempt to amplify a small orchestra to replicate a larger orchestra and widen the interest in classical music. *Time* magazine called him the Evil Knievel of classical music.

Revenaugh told me that I was making a mistake by moving back to Minnesota, but I knew that it would be selfish of me to continue towards a dead end in a performing career and create a financial burden for my parents. I applied to transfer to Macalester and was accepted for the incoming junior year in the fall of 1996. I began to prepare for my return to Minnesota and decided to play a recital for some friends on March 26, 1996. It was a great opportunity to reconnect with Bill, so I invited him. He replied:

Dear Lawrence:

I certainly do remember you, with much admiration. I am lecturing in the South on [March] 26th, and I'm afraid it's a little bit too late even

to attempt to round up an audience but I wish
you all the best.

With cordial regards,
Wm. F. Buckley, Jr.

I could feel that the connection with Bill was tenuous at
best and that, given his busy schedule, arranging another meeting would be difficult, if not impossible. As I said goodbye to
New York that spring and moved back to Minnesota, it felt
more permanent, like a farewell.

Chapter 10

IN THE WILDERNESS

*Every prophet has to come from civilization, but
every prophet has to go into the wilderness. He
must have a strong impression of a complex society
and all that it has to give, and then he must serve
a period of isolation and meditation. This is the
process by which psychic dynamite is made.*

—Winston Churchill

When I enrolled at Macalester College as a third-year
student the college made an exception and allowed
Yakov to become a visiting faculty member so he
could be my professor. It was wonderful to be reunited with him.
I had declared a double major in political science and music.
Macalester was, and is still known as, a very liberal college. As I
got to know the professors in the political science department I
would mention my meeting with William F. Buckley, Jr. They
smiled politely but didn't exactly understand my reverence for
him. One professor had a gigantic poster of Karl Marx on his
wall and taught "Developmental Politics," which focused on

third-world countries and how imperialism and colonialism had stymied their growth and opportunities.

At some point that fall semester I became very interested in Richard Nixon and was reading a number of his books, including a memoir in which he wrote about being "in the wilderness" between his time as vice president and president. I started to view my return to Minnesota as my "wilderness" and realized that I would need to begin looking at a plan to return to New York. I focused on my studies and the piano but the calling of entrepreneurship was loud and at times deafening.

I stayed in touch with Revenaugh, who was mostly in Berkeley. In the spring of 1997, he asked me to bring his invention, the lower lid, a reflective graphite panel mirroring the upper lid of the grand piano, to Montreal so that Martha Argerich could use it. Radu Lupu, the esteemed Romanian pianist, had recently used it with the Minnesota Orchestra, so it was just across the river from St. Paul at Orchestra Hall in Minneapolis. The lower lid gave the piano the look of a butterfly and Revenaugh had proven that it made the sound of the piano more stereophonic and propelled it farther into the auditorium by scooping up sound that would otherwise dissipate underneath the piano just as the top lid directed sound to the audience. This prototype was kept in a bicycle box and I was to simply check it at the airport, fly to Montreal, and bring the box to the hotel. As I packed the bicycle box the hinges that connected the lower lid to the piano wouldn't fit, so I put the hinges in my suitcase and checked it at the airport along with the bicycle box. When I landed in Montreal the bicycle box arrived, but my suitcase didn't. All hell broke loose when I saw Revenaugh at the hotel and he realized that I didn't have the hinges. When things calmed down Revenaugh's solution was to tape the lower lid, which weighed about ten pounds, onto the piano and have me hold it up under the piano so Argerich could use the lower lid in her rehearsal with the Montreal Symphony and conductor Charles Dutoit. Here I was, twenty-one, holding up the lower lid under the great Martha Argerich's piano with my elbow on Maestro Dutoit's podium with members of the Montreal Symphony giggling at the sight of it. I held onto the lid through all the shoulder pain and reminded myself that POWs went through much worse. People had gone their entire lives never hearing Argerich play and here I was under her piano while she played Prokofiev and Bartok!

The hinges arrived the next day, Argerich agreed to use the lower lid, and the concert was a great success. Argerich and Revenaugh had met in 1969 and hadn't seen one another in quite a few years, so this was a reunion. Argerich was alluringly charismatic, and for me as a pianist, this time was the culmination of a lifetime goal to hear her in person. She had battled two bouts of malignant melanoma and had been treated with an experimental vaccine from the John Wayne Cancer Institute in California. She was now in remission.

That year I also arranged a tour of Europe in a matter of months for an organization I founded called the International Association of Young Artists. The tour took place from July 7 to August 14, 1997, and I invited twelve young artists from leading conservatories on Cunard Line's *Queen Elizabeth 2*, sailing from New York to Southampton, England; to perform chamber music in luxury hotels in Switzerland, Germany, and London; and then to perform again on the *Queen Elizabeth 2* from Southampton, England back to New York. I even got local Minnesota arts patron Dolly Fiterman to contribute to it along with Sotheby's and Montblanc. I sit in admiration of my younger self when I look back at my productivity and the fact that I faxed more than one hundred hotels pitching the tour on a few months' notice. I had absolutely no marketing or PR experience and cold-called and pitched everyone, leveraging relationships at Steinway & Sons, where Peter Goodrich put me in contact with Cunard Line, resulting in the roundtrip on the *Queen Elizabeth 2*. Of course, my parents' generosity played a major role as well with them underwriting a significant portion of the tour when I realized that I had fallen short of the needed fundraising. Their support never wavered and continuously gave me confidence that I was on the right road.

The lower-lid encounter with Argerich and the European tour marked a turning point for me and made me realize that a career as an impresario working with artists, producing events, and promoting classical music was what I was born to do.

My time in the Minnesota wilderness turned out to be productive and transformative. I lived at home, practiced the piano, and worked on my senior thesis on détente policy. With graduation approaching in the spring of 1998, I knew that my focus had to be on returning to New York. How I would get there would depend entirely on me since my parents couldn't subsidize the move back, especially after my two years at Macalester and the European tour. At graduation I perused the program and came upon the name David Bell, a member of the Macalester board of trustees and president of advertising agency Bozell Worldwide; I made a note to write him a letter.

In the summer I started to make a list of everyone I would meet with on a one-month trip to New York with the aim of landing a job and moving back. The list included Peter Gelb, the head of Sony Classical; David Bell at Bozell Worldwide; and, of course, at the top of the list, William F. Buckley, Jr.

I wrote to Bill on August 31, 1998:

Dear Mr. Buckley:

It has been quite some time since I have written. In 1995, I had the honor of meeting and
performing on the piano at your home in
Manhattan. This memory has stayed with me
and always shall. Much has taken place over the
past three years, including my graduation from
Macalester College (definitely not on your list
of colleges!), the founding of the International
Association of Young Artists (IAYA) in 1996
and the production of its subsequent tour in
1997 (see programme). IAYA was founded to
address the future of classical music and the
role of the young artist.

My goals are manifold. Over the next several
decades I plan to make classical music into the
success story in the commercial arena that conservatism has been in the political arena. Who
better to go to for advice than one of the fathers
of conservatism? If not for you, conservatism
would not be the force that it has been during
this century and will be during the next.

Mr. Buckley, please understand how much the
response to my letter and the subsequent meeting in 1995 meant to me. The meeting left in
me the impression of a great statesman this
country is so privileged to have. Through your
actions you are undoubtedly one of the few

individuals today who evoke the quintessential qualities of a consummate gentleman.

I will be in Manhattan from October 15 through November 15 and hope you have some time available during which we can meet. I thank you in advance for having taken the time to read this letter and look forward to hearing from you. I remain,

Respectfully yours,
Lawrence Perelman

I sent the letter off to *National Review* and once again used FedEx to guarantee it would be received.

On September 9, I got a call from Frances Bronson! The familiar English accent that had put down the phone on me in 1994 simply stated, "He wants to see you." My heart raced.

We set the meeting for 5:30 p.m. on November 2, 1998, at 73 East 73rd Street. I couldn't believe it. I was back *in* and once again couldn't wait to walk up to that Narnian door and ring the doorbell.

My parents were supportive of this month-long trip to New York where we all hoped I would find my way forward. They were excited about Bill agreeing to meet with me again but couldn't help looking at me as the dreamer that was burrowing into their retirement fund with his crazy ventures. Looking back, the uncertainty facing me didn't weigh as much as thinking about it now does. I was going back to New York on spec and meeting with people to see who just might introduce me to someone who might be interested in hiring me. I was twenty-two and had great ambitions to make classical music a more formidable part of the cultural firmament, but who would truly see something in me and believe in it? Who would be willing to invest in me and give me a real opportunity right off the street and with no real tangible experience beyond producing a luxurious European tour, an encounter with Martha Argerich, and being a sidekick to a classical music entrepreneur who invented a lower lid for the grand piano? Perhaps I was somewhat naive but that naiveté also fueled my vision and purpose. I was young but was also confident and thought I could really contribute my ideas to my artform. I believed that people should take notice of my ideas and consider my advice. It was so clear to me that classical music was relevant and one of the greatest achievements in human history. Few contributions to the world have had such a profound effect on the mind and soul as listening to the greatest compositions ever produced by the human mind. The fact that someone could go through life never hearing these works was staggering to me and I wanted everyone to pay attention to these creations.

I boarded the plane on October 15, 1998, bound for New York with all of this eagerness, energy, and ambition. Little did I know what awaited me and that Bill was in search of someone just like me.

Chapter 11

"HE WANTS TO SEE YOU"

He wants to see you.

—FRANCES BRONSON, SEPTEMBER 9, 1998

f playing for Bill in 1995 was a defining moment for me, my second visit was even more crucial. Getting through the door once is hard, but the second time, much harder. It had been three-and-a-half years since my first visit. I wasn't sure what piqued his interest and Frances Bronson's cryptic words, "He wants to see you," didn't give me a clue. A copy of the letter I sent to Bill on August 31, 1998, was retrieved from the Yale University archive in 2010 by my friend Linda Bridges, one of *National Review*'s most respected longtime editors who in Bill's final years served as the repository and hub for all things Buckley with saint-like devotion. On the letter is a note in Bill's barely legible handwriting: "Frances can you find a half hour for him?" On the upper-left-hand corner is my phone number in legible handwriting. Then there's "Nov. 2, 5:30, 73," which translated to November 2, 5:30 p.m. at 73 East 73rd Street. He circled one word in red: "advice." It's these sentences that seem to have gotten his attention:

> My goals are manifold. Over the next several decades I plan to make classical music into the success story in the commercial arena that conservatism has been in the political arena. Who better to go to for *advice* [emphasis added] than one of the fathers of conservatism? If not for you, conservatism would not be the force that it has been during this century and will be during the next.

I knew nothing of his plans when I approached 73 East 73rd Street on November 2. I rang the doorbell for the second time in my life. This time I brought a box of five Davidoff cigars, graduating from orange juice to a real gift. There I was again standing in front of those magisterial iron doors leading into the most amazing home I had seen in my life. The doors opened and there was William F. Buckley, Jr., for the second time in my life. He invited me in. Once again, we walked past the harpsichord, down the marble hallway towards the sweeping spiral staircase, and to the right into the brightly lit library with its sumptuous red glow. We sat down and he offered me a drink. Now twenty-two, I accepted a glass of wine.

Bill asked for a recap of my activities since our first meeting in 1995. I recounted the decision to leave New York and transfer to Macalester College. I explained how I survived my professor with the Karl Marx poster. More important, I told him about my work related to music and producing the European tour as well as meeting Martha Argerich. I stressed how much I wanted to move back to New York to work on classical music becoming more visible in mainstream media and to achieve my dream of starting a cable channel dedicated to the performing arts.

After my monologue of a few minutes, I recall Bill saying, "You've spoken, now let me speak." He continued, "Recently, I had lunch with my friend Schuyler Chapin, the commissioner of Cultural Affairs for the City of New York. He told me that New York City is re-introducing music education in its public schools. I *never* knew that music education had been out of the city schools since the 1970s." I listened intently as Bill elaborated: "I'm curious to know how the absence of music education in New York City's public schools affected the individuals who attended school as well as the city's musical life. Or think of it another way, what does good music do for you? I need someone to research this subject for me. Would you be interested?"

I was stunned. Was William F. Buckley, Jr., asking me to do a research project for him? I continued and asked, "Do you mean do research for you?"

Bill smiled and said, "I have a research foundation—the Historical Research Foundation—and would like to give you a six-month grant to answer this question for me."

My shock perpetuated, "What do you mean by a grant?"

Bill continued, "The grant is $25,000. All you need to do is write a proposal. If it looks good, I'll push it through the committee. You can move back to New York in January [1999], work for me on this project, and pursue all of your other endeavors in parallel."

In a daze, I continued, "Mr. Buckley, I don't know what to say. Thank you for thinking of me for this. I'm honored."

He grinned and simply said, "Go write the proposal."

Our meeting was over in thirty minutes. This time the piano remained untouched. It was all business. I got my things and thanked him profusely. He walked me down the hall, back to the iron doors, opened the door, smiled, and said, "I look forward to reading the proposal."

Tears began to roll down my cheeks as I walked out. I called my parents while standing in front of Bill's doors. My mom picked up the phone and I said, "I think William F. Buckley, Jr., just offered me a research grant!"

So many things had transpired in that meeting in such a short period of time. He offered me a grant right there on the spot! Who does that? I was on a high that I had never experienced. The fact that he said it was basically a done deal was unbelievable—$25,000 was enough to live on for six to nine months in New York! What if I ran out of money? What would I do? Those were all questions for later. Now, I had to write the proposal and ensure that the plan to return to New York would become a reality.

I crafted a two-page proposal over the next two days and sent it off to *National Review* on November 9, 1998. Here's an excerpt:

> I am interested in a $25,000 grant to conduct six months of research in New York City beginning in January 1999 on the following question:
>
> How has the twenty-five year absence of music education in New York City public schools—a program recently reinstated—affected both the individuals who attended the public schools during the period and the city's musical life?
>
> My first order of business will be to lay the groundwork for the research by understanding

exactly what the function was of music education program that existed in the public school
system twenty-five years ago before being aban-
doned and exactly what has been reinstated...

The twenty-five year absence may also have
affected the city's musical life (i.e., the entire
population's musical tastes, what is played on
the radio, what is being sold and purchased in
record stores, etc.).

As classical music becomes less of a factor in
the lives of most Americans I feel it is necessary
to learn whether this is partly due to the lack
of exposure a child has to *good* music while
attending school.

Once again, I sent the letter to Bill via FedEx. And the waiting began, again.

The meeting with Bill was the centerpiece of my trip, but I
also met with David Bell at Bozell Worldwide, and Peter Gelb,
the president of Sony Classical, who would go on to become the
general manager of the Metropolitan Opera. My meeting with
David Bell was a lot of fun and the Bozell offices were where the
Tom Hanks movie *Big* was filmed. When I met with Bill a few
days before, I had asked if Bozell Worldwide had any connection to his brother-in-law Brent Bozell, who had ghost-written
Barry Goldwater's *Conscience of a Conservative*. It turned out
that Brent Bozell's father had indeed started the Bozell agency.
David was very supportive of my ideas for classical music's reju-
venation and encouraged me to stay in touch, which we did.
Peter Gelb told me that his door was open when I completed

my research project saying, "Good for Bill" when I told him what he had offered me.

It was an amazing trip to New York with what seemed like doors opening for me left and right.

I returned home on November 15, and a letter from Bill was waiting for me:

> November 13, 1998
>
> Dear Larry:
>
> I think your application is beautifully worded and wonderfully thoughtful. I have set the wheels in motion and you should hear back from Mr. Dino Pionzio.
>
> With warm regards,
> Wm. F. Buckley, Jr.

I was ecstatic, yet nervous. "When will I hear back? Who is Dino Pionzio?" During our meeting, Bill had mentioned starting the research in January. That was less than two months away. It takes time to find an apartment. I had to book a flight back to New York. There were so many things to do. My parents were apprehensive but, as always, supportive.

A few days later I received a certified letter from Dino Pionzio of the Historical Research Foundation:

> November 17, 1998
>
> Dear Mr. Perelman:
>
> I am pleased to advise you that, on the strong recommendation of Mr. Buckley and the

support of [Evan G. Galbraith], the Project Committee of the Historical Research Foundation has agreed to make a total of $25,000 available to you for the purposes outlined in your letter of November 9, 1998.

Accordingly, enclosed is a check for $15,000 to get you on under way. We will send you the balance of $10,000 when the project is completed, or before, if the need can be demonstrated....

Please keep Mr. Buckley closely advised of your project and he, in turn, will inform the Committee.

Respectfully,
Dino J. Pionzio
President

Barely two weeks after my meeting with Bill on November 5, I had the first installment of my grant: $15,000. I was speechless.

I was in a daze, and my parents were amazingly proud. It seemed as though their investment in my crazy ambitions had paid off. This was an endorsement of their son from someone they revered. Maybe, just maybe, I would find my way in New York with the guidance of William F. Buckley, Jr.

My missionary zeal for classical music mirrored Bill's for conservatism and, as it turned out, classical music. Our two comets would collide on a fateful day in September 1998 when my letter arrived at *National Review* and he had just had lunch with Schuyler Chapin. It's very likely that had Bill not had lunch with Chapin or my letter hadn't arrived when it did, I would never have received that call from Frances. It was Bill's insatiable appetite for learning and his unending curiosity which made all of this possible.

Here was Bill, the American impresario, taking a completely fresh mind like me and throwing him into the mix, and giving him an unthinkable opportunity. Bill was willing to take risks as he illustrated time and time again. My role was small in the grand scheme of things but it was part of the world that Bill created. He believed that classical music should be a vital part of our society, so he was going to mentor a young man who was passionate, as he was mentored by Willi Schlamm, and others, when he was in his twenties and launching *National Review*. I believe that he wanted to replicate the opportunities he received and to see how others would go on to change the world. This was his generosity and trust at their fullest.

Bill's qualities are what are missing in our society today. Each of us needs to emulate these, and as we do, we'll find that our society will become more trusting, more willing to interact, and ultimately more united. Bill's ability to change the life of a complete stranger is a lesson for all of us. It wasn't charity, it was an endorsement, and an invitation to become part of his circle and world. Milton Friedman said that Bill's greatest quality was his friendship, but I would go one step further and say that his trust was his greatest quality and allowed him to be the ultimate friend and mentor to not only his friends and protégés, but to his nation.

Chapter 12

LUNCH AT PAONE'S

Perhaps you'll play a little Mozart for me.

—William F. Buckley, Jr., to
me, December 9, 1998

December 9, 1998

Dear Larry:

I was deeply impressed by you yet again, as you
will have gathered. And enormously enthusiastic about the project, which of course will go
hand in hand with your own project. I have
already spoken with Schuyler Chapin and he is
willing to meet with you and I know it will be
extremely illuminating. Make a date soon for
the end of January as I leave early in February
for Switzerland for one of my book writing

expeditions and I am very anxious to see you. Perhaps you will play a little Mozart for me.

With warm regards,
Wm. F. Buckley, Jr.

I moved back to New York at the beginning of March 1999, since it took some time to find an apartment and make what I hoped would be a permanent move to New York. Bill was leaving for his "book writing expedition" in early February and wanted me to meet Schuyler Chapin as soon as possible. Therefore, I flew to New York for a meeting on February 1, 1999, with Bill and Chapin at Paone's, a quintessential 1960s-style Italian restaurant that had frescoes, chianti in the whicker bottles, and a dessert tray rivaling anything one can find today. Paone's was long known as a *National Review* favorite and closed its doors in 2008 after decades in operation. That lunch was memorable not only for sitting at the table with Bill and Chapin, New York City's commissioner of Cultural Affairs, but also for the fact that I was fifty years their junior. I took myself very seriously, but looking back now and seeing my twenty-two-year -old self at the table with these two men is still something very special. Bill was charming as always and introduced me to Chapin as a pianist, entrepreneur, and researcher looking for the answer to his question, "What does the lack of art cost you?" He asked Chapin to give me some background on how New York City was working with the Annenberg Foundation to secure the return of arts education in city schools. Chapin offered to make introductions for me to key players in the city's administration, including Deputy Mayor Ninfa Segarra, who also served on the Board of Education and would become the city's last president of the Board of Education after supporting its abolition in 2002 when the State of New York returned control over city schools to the mayor.

Chapin said his door would be open anytime I had questions or required help with visits to schools and arranging interviews. I don't remember what I had for lunch, but the dessert tray stands out with the largest goblet of chocolate pudding I had ever seen topped off with whipped cream. As the cart made its way over, Bill surveyed it and looked over at me. My eyes were focused on the pudding and Bill said, "Go ahead and have one."

My head was spinning as I realized that Bill had basically plucked me out of a crop of young people eager to be mentored by him and thrust me into a power lunch in Midtown Manhattan. I quickly learned that this was Bill's modus operandi: If you could impress him and those around him then the opportunities would multiply quickly.

This was a passion project for Bill, and it allowed him to revel in the arts, especially classical music or "good music" as he called it. Bill had dedicated an entire thirty-minute episode of *Firing Line* to learning the Bach concerto for the Phoenix Symphony. It's available on YouTube, made possible by the Hoover Institution, which acquired the *Firing Line* archive. There's Bill as I had never seen him, performing Bach on a harpsichord with an orchestra and conductor. The look on Bill's face is nearly heavenly as though he is being observed in prayer.

**William F. Buckley, Jr. practicing Bach on the harpsichord
in Phoenix, Arizona in 1989 during the filming of
Firing Line. Courtesy of the Hoover Institution.**

Prior to the performance he is interviewed by Schuyler
Chapin. The idea that a decade later I would be sitting and having lunch with them both holds even more significance for me
with this added context and the interactions between these two
gentlemen. The lovely discourse and discussion between Bill
and Chapin rarely finds its way into the public square today.
"Rarely" is perhaps too generous, since one will hardly find a
program dedicating thirty minutes to classical music and a discussion about the state of the orchestra landscape in America.
Today people will often argue that things were different in the
1980s and 1990s and that the European roots of the American
public were stronger then and hence classical music was more
relevant. I believe that people like Bill were the ones defining
culture and therefore people recognized classical music's importance. His generation believed that the humanities were just
that, the achievement of human beings and not of one race or

ethnicity. To Bill, Bach was divine and not merely the creation of a German man who couldn't relate to today's inner-city school children. The entire argument that classical music is elitist is a figment of imagination and not based on fact. Ultimately, throughout the world one sees many examples of average citizens in countries with no ethnic, religious, or cultural connection to Bach, Beethoven, Mozart, or Tchaikovsky celebrating those composers, and so many more, in myriad ways. Here are just three examples: 1) The Suzuki Method was developed in Japan and has spread around the world. 2) Violinist Isaac Stern traveled to China in 1979 spreading Western classical music not long after the Cultural Revolution. His work is widely credited with making China a classical music powerhouse. 3) Venezuela's El Sistema, founded in 1975, has given millions of children government funded music education and produced countless orchestral musicians and many international artists. Although many, including myself, see the last example as a propaganda tool of a repressive regime, El Sistema has remained in place regardless of political party since it was founded in 1975.

Bill chose to dedicate airtime to Bach, his pursuit of performing with an orchestra, and a discussion about the state of orchestras in America, because he had the power and will to do so. Bill was the impresario of *Firing Line* and could decide what he programmed, and in the process the program was singular in the annals of American television history for promulgating culture of this level to the masses.

Chapin, with a career in the world of performing arts, leaned leftward in his politics, and his friendship with Bill was emblematic of that era. People were likely to have political disagreements but would also find common ground. Chapin served in Rudy Giuliani's mayoral administration, which at that time was viewed as liberal by many of the Right, yet celebrated for its positions on crime that led to a Renaissance in America's largest city.

As Bill and I walked away from the restaurant, I asked him about his thoughts on the Clinton impeachment hearings that were underway. Bill was circumspect and said he had no idea if Clinton would be removed from office. We bid farewell until he would return to New York from Switzerland in March, at which point I would be moved into my new apartment and ready to start my research project.

Chapter 13

"CALL ME 'BILL'"

Call me "Bill."

—William F. Buckley, Jr., to me, March 29, 1999

A s I settled into my tiny apartment on the Upper West Side, I received an invitation to the Buckley residence, known as "the maisonette" to invited guests, for a dinner on Monday, March 29 at 6:30 p.m. *National Review* editors would gather at the maisonette on 73rd Street for the "fortnightly dinner" and celebrate the new issue of the magazine, which was published every two weeks. Joining the publisher, senior editors, and select staff from *National Review* including Linda Bridges, Priscilla Buckley, (Bill's sister), Richard Brookhiser, Larry Kudlow, Rich Lowry, and Jay Nordlinger were guests of honor, like Bill's friend Henry Kissinger as well as friends of Bill's wife Patricia T. Buckley, "Pat" to her friends, who was one of New York's most important socialites.

I was excited to be invited to a dinner party and had no idea what to expect. Now twenty-three, I entered the maisonette as a complete newcomer. This time a butler answered the door and asked for my coat. Nearly everyone was decades older than me, except for maybe one junior editor or intern who was chosen to attend so that the next generation could benefit from what amounted to one of the last New York salons. I walked down the now familiar corridor, past the harpsichord and the sweeping staircase, and into the red library where the guests congregated for drinks. Hors d'oeuvres were shrimp cocktail, slices of salami, and Bill's favorite concoction: Ritz crackers, peanut butter, and bacon bits. Bill loved peanut butter so much that Red Wing peanut butter gave him a lifetime supply with a private label for having written in a column that it was the best. "Buckley's Best Peanut Butter" was on his private label along with his quote, "It is quite simply incomparable" along with his signature in classic red pen. He once quipped, and I paraphrase, that "if peanut butter was as scarce as caviar, it would be served at Buckingham Palace by the Queen of England." Bill appeared as if from nowhere and greeted me, "Hey, buddy." I soon learned that this was his "go to" greeting. We chatted for barely a minute before he moved on with lightning speed to speak with nearly every guest. Working a room is tough business and if you get caught in one conversation you've lost the opportunity to connect with everyone. He was a master at connecting and of efficiency, so much so that he made everyone feel like they had his attention.

The library was getting full, and after about thirty minutes we adjourned to the spectacular dining room, which, much like the room I had visited to play piano, seemed like it was 1,000 square feet. On display alongside a table on one of the walls was the Presidential Medal of Freedom, which President George H.W. Bush had bestowed upon Bill in 1991. The two large tables, each seating twelve, were set in a manner I had never seen in my life. There were three or four forks and knives on each side of a formal stack of two beautiful porcelain plates that sat atop a charger plate. Name cards in perfect handwritten italics were placed on each plate. There were ornate red carved crystal bowls with slices of lemon floating in the water; I later learned these were finger bowls for dipping one's fingers between courses. The centerpieces were floral arrangements, bottles of wine sat open on top of wine holders, and small narrow bowls held a handful of cigarettes with the initials PTB on the cigarette paper wrapping. The personalized cigarettes were an anachronism even in 1999 and the initials were, of course, for Patricia T. Buckley.

Pat knew how to make an entrance and was always ready for her close-up. Men dominated the room and posture immediately improved when she arrived. Formality ensued. She was responsible for all the glitz and leopard skin around the house. She was intimidating and knew it. Her friends were a Who's Who of fashion from Oscar de la Renta to Valentino, as well as the 1960s and 1970s club scene where she reportedly partied with Warhol and others at Studio 54. Members of her circle veered left in their politics, and her "ladies who lunch" friends ran the galas and benefits of all the major Manhattan institutions. She co-chaired the Met Museum's Gala for years with her friend Nan Kempner. She was a force of nature in her own right and her sly wit could dig deep for the uninitiated. She approached me that first evening with a combination of a grin and scowl; I said "hello" and barely registered on her radar. She walked along in her aloof and elegant way. We were all asked to be seated. The banter between guests continued at the tables. There was a warmth and feel of friendship all around.

Bill sat at the head of a table at the far end of the room, which was mostly populated with *National Review* editors. Pat sat at the head of a table at the other end of the room with other writers, friends, and non-*National Review*-affiliated guests. I was seated at Pat's table. The Buckleys were across the room from each other but would occasionally announce things to each other punctuated by the nickname "Ducky," which they both used for each other. This was all very foreign to me but was obviously normal to everyone else. Seated to my right was Peter Duchin, part of the Duchin big band dynasty having continued in the tradition of his father Eddy. Mr. Duchin asked me what my connection was to the Buckleys and I told him that I had just received a grant from Bill's foundation and moved back to New York to do some research on music education. We chatted, and throughout the evening the wine flowed, and the courses were served by wait staff formally visiting each guest with gigantic platters for each course. It was magical to sit amongst these guests in the rarefied air of New York's intellectual hub and society. It was also completely surreal and cinematic.

During dessert, I felt a tap on my left shoulder. It was Bill, "Larry, I'm going to ask you to say a few words about your research to the guests. Prepare to introduce yourself and say a little something." "OK, of course," I replied. I hadn't had too much to drink, but enough to feel as though this was a real surprise and thought I was ill prepared. I then heard Bill say something to Duchin about offering "a rebuttal" to what I was going to say. What was he talking about? Rebuttal?

A few minutes later I could hear Bill's voice asking everyone to quiet down. "Larry Perelman, would you please say a few words about your research project?" All of this stated in Bill's singular accent. I thought to myself, "Is this a mock *Firing Line*? I just started this project. I haven't done much at all! Compose yourself, Larry." I then started to mumble something, and Bill's voice rose, "Please stand up!" I stood up, and all of the guests' eyes were fixed on me. I introduced myself and proceeded to give them a brief description of the project, explaining that the "lack of music education in New York City public schools had cost millions of students the opportunity to learn about the greatness of classical music." I mentioned how thankful I was to Mr. Buckley for the opportunity. I really wasn't sure if I made any sense but it was an extraordinary moment for me and the fact that Bill had just thrown me into the deep end. "Thank you, Larry. Peter Duchin, would you please offer a rebuttal?" Duchin smiled and stood up. He was as ill prepared as I but also experienced at these kinds of things. He said something about how music education is only part of the equation, but I can't completely recall given my overwhelmed state at speaking in front of that group at Bill's request.

Within minutes of completing our comments, Bill announced that dinner was over and that there would be after-dinner drinks in the living room. Some headed home as others moved into the living room. I followed along and met a few more people that evening, including *National Review* publisher Jack Fowler and *National Review* chairman Dusty Rhodes. Bill was sitting and speaking with a few editors when I walked up and said, "Mr. Buckley, thank you so much for inviting me tonight." He looked at me and said, "Call me Bill." He then invited me to attend the filming of *Firing Line* a few days later on March 31, 1999. To say I was in a state of awe would be a massive understatement.

* * *

I soon understood that this had all been an initiation process, which ended that night nearly four years after we first met. Bill had been a member of Skull & Bones, the storied Yale secret society, and also a member of the CIA. I learned many years later that Dino Pionzio, the president of the Historical Research Foundation, was a very important member of the CIA and also a Yalie, and an alum of Skull & Bones. With the statement, "Call me Bill," I was officially in the circle of trust. As I left that evening and walked in the crisp spring Manhattan air, I couldn't believe what lay ahead of me. However, looking back I now realize that Bill really saw something in me and a potential to achieve things. There's no question I exhibited persistence but what I never did was cross the line to become annoying or hounding. His letters, the invitation to play for him, the grant, and now this invitation to his home were columns in a grand structure taking shape, structured by a man who would soon become one of the most important people in my life. I was among many who had experienced Bill's largesse and mentorship. It came naturally to him, the role of mentor and impresario. He would always be looking for the opportunity to create opportunities for others. This was an incredible virtue that endeared him to so many.

Chapter 14

WHAT DOES THE LACK OF ART COST YOU?

MR. BUCKLEY: Well now, I have heard you complain that New York City schools simply stopped exposing students to music for twenty-five years.

MR. CHAPIN: Twenty-five years, and that is, of course, now, thank God, over because the arts—music, theater, dance, poetry, and painting and sculpture—are back in the schools, back in all of them by September of 1999. Arts curriculum is back. We had a generation in this city, two generations actually, without any arts education. And the audiences in theaters and in museums began to be noted for being grey-haired instead of youthful. And when you cut out the education system, you're cutting out the most important introduction of the arts to children.

MR. BUCKLEY: Well, speak to us of what damage was done. If we go twenty-five years without teaching the public school children and exposing them to music or arts, what becomes palpable after that?

—*FIRING LINE*, MARCH 31, 1999

* * *

I entered the HBO Studios off Bryant Park on March 31, 1999, for the taping of *Firing Line*. As I made my way to the studio, I looked for Bill and soon found him chatting with Schuyler Chapin and Rosalyn Tureck. To my elation the episode was tailormade for me: "Is Good Music Going Under?" The topic of my research was popping up everywhere from the fortnightly dinner and now *Firing Line*. Bill's ability to influence was staggering since he could simultaneously draw attention to a topic in his magazine, television program and, as he called it, his "thrice weekly column." I sucked up every ounce of being in Bill's presence and in the company of two legends whom he also called friends. The episode touched on the topic of my research and focused heartily on the question of classical music's odds of survival in the cultural firmament. At one point Bill posits the following to Chapin, "But assume in a laboratory test you've got a hundred twelve-year-olds and you put them in a room, and you turn off the lights. And for two hours a week you play the great works of the nineteenth century. Okay, three months go by, and you set out to find out what percentage of those hundred students now enjoy it." This was Bill basically imposing on the broader public the Great Elm music listening experience he and his siblings were subjected to as children. In theory it was a wonderful idea, but in reality, as I would find out during the course of my research, it wasn't at all what was going on in New York City Public Schools.

William F. Buckley, Jr., Rosalyn Tureck, and Schuyler Chapin on the set of *Firing Line* on March 31, 1999. Courtesy of the Hoover Institution.

Bill's column was called "On the Right." It was a platform on which to muse about anything he wanted and distributed to hundreds of American newspapers. The well was deep and Bill went to it every few days for ideas. That same week I received an email from Bill with his most recent column. Once again, it mirrored my research topic and further confirmed how seriously Bill was taking this question. The article was titled "What does the lack of art cost you?" It delved into the details of Chapin's work with the Giuliani administration to reintroduce arts education in New York City Public Schools and Bill's

focus on music education since that was his real interest in the
matter. Here's the column in its entirety:

> FROM UNIVERSAL PRESS
> SYNDICATE FOR IMMEDIATE
> RELEASE DATED: 4/2/99
>
> ON THE RIGHT by William F. Buckley, Jr.
>
> WHAT DOES THE LACK
> OF ART COST YOU?
>
> The question comes up more or less perpetu-
> ally. Is classical music going down the drain?
> Some of the indices are wonderfully buoy-
> ant: There are 1,800 symphony orchestras
> today compared to 1,200 20 years ago. On
> the other hand, classical music record sales
> were down by 10 percent last year. Even the
> boosters acknowledge that one-third of seats at
> good-music events are empty, though they are
> quick to remind you that our halls contain two
> or three times as many seats as the symphony
> halls of the 18th century.
>
> A development in New York City is of special
> interest to music pathologists. In 1975, the
> New York City public schools ended all forms
> of art instruction. No more music apprecia-
> tion, no bands, no dance, no art classes: It was a
> great Philistine glacial inundation, and it lasted
> for 22 years.

In 1997, Mayor Giuliani, himself an ardent music-lover, ended the awful blight. Eighty-five schools have now begun the restoration of art programs, enthusiastically egged on by New York's commissioner of culture, Schuyler Chapin, a starstruck music lover who once headed up the Metropolitan Opera Company and served as dean of arts at Columbia University. The auspices, in other words, are ideal.

The interesting question?

What about the people who were deprived? To use round numbers, let us say that 25 million people went through 12 years of learning in New York City receiving no exposure of any kind to music. Applying the Poundian modification ("Education is for those who will not do without it"), let us suppose that one-tenth of those students went and searched out music on their own. Another tenth (let us assume) got it at home, like the religious training the ACLU is so enthusiastic about. That still leaves millions who never got it. If they stumbled across it on the radio or on television, what did they do? Switch immediately to another channel?

Both Mayor Giuliani and Commissioner Chapin sing like nightingales when asked about music. But should one stop to ask: What does the absence of an exposure to classical music actually *do* to somebody? We know color-blind people (specifically, I know two) who are presumably deprived of the pleasure of viewing Fauvist permutations in art. If there are 15 million graduates of New York City public schools who have never heard the last duet in Aida, or Beethoven's 9th Symphony, what is the exact nature of their deprivation? What does it do to them? Anything? If so, what?

It is an engrossing question. We know what someone suffers from if he/she fails to learn to read. It is hideously obvious what we suffer from if blind, or deaf. We lie down early in life with the maxim that the absence of a cultural education is crippling. But the raw material has surely never been more conveniently available than, courtesy of New York City, it now is. Men and women between the ages of 20 and 45, millions of them. How are they distinguishable from their seniors, who were taught art?

It is too easy to say that special pleasures are there for those who have eyes to see and ears to hear. Is it a loss of potential pleasure we are speaking of? That only? Or are foreshortened aesthetic sensibilities in other ways costly? If you never responded with excitement to an hour with Verdi, does that mean that you will be less aware of—what? The sound of the lark? The beauty of the spring? The pleasures of Lincoln's rhetoric? And how do these deprivations combine to lessen your value as a citizen?

Do they combine at all? Do you die younger?
Older? Fatter? Richer?

The schoolchildren of New York owe a great
deal to Mr. Giuliani and the overseers who
have given them back what we like to think of
as their patrimony. But we need to make the
value of what they have now clearer. And we
need to ask, sorrowfully, why it is that a city
so large does without a noncommercial radio
station that gives good music around the clock.
Is the diminished demand for music over the
air a fallout of the 22 years of neglect?

We know of a young scholar who is poking
into these questions. When he has the answers,
you will have them from this space five minutes later.

I was the "young scholar" to which Bill referred to at the end
of his column. Everything was very real now and moving at a fast
clip. The article motivated me to begin my research and soon I
met with Schuyler Chapin at the New York City Department
of Cultural Affairs. Chapin made good on his earlier promise
to arrange introductions and set up meetings. He was very
enthusiastic and saw a kindred spirit in me as a someone from
the classical music world. I aspired to emulate Chapin some-
day since he had attained the highest reaches in my industry.
Chapin asked me to stay in contact and update him from time
to time on the progress of my research.

I visited a number of schools to see firsthand what was
meant by "arts" education and whether music education was

part of the mix in the city's aim to reintroduce arts education. Bill's question was built on an assumption that the reintroduction of arts education in New York meant that all school children would now be going through the experiences similar to the Great Elm music appreciation listening sessions with Bach's Goldberg Variations or Beethoven's symphonies being played for children of all walks of life stretching to every corner of New York City. The reality was quite the opposite, and when I visited schools I saw that what was defined as "art" depended on the students, teachers, and school districts. The schools received funds from the city and Annenberg Foundation, but those came with no requirements to make music or specific artistic subjects available to schoolchildren.

As my research progressed, Bill invited me to attend any *Firing Line* tapings that interested me. I took him up on this several times in 1999 not knowing that this would be the program's final year. He also made clear that my research should go hand in hand with pursuing my other interests in promoting classical music and doing so through other projects.

From time to time invitations to special events would come my way including to the forty-fifth anniversary of *National Review*. The gala took place on World Yacht's Princess liner with an evening dinner sail around Manhattan. Giving one of the speeches, Tom Wolfe remarked that if the boat went down, then with it would go "most of the conservative movement." There was laughter and some trepidation. I recall Charlton Heston and Rush Limbaugh among the hundreds of guests. Limbaugh was obsessed with Bill and did a worthy impression of him during his radio program. Bill recounted during a sail to Oyster Bay that Limbaugh showed up at a fortnightly dinner with a magnum of Petrus worth more than $10,000 and box of H. Upmann pre-Castro Cuban cigars, again valued in the thousands of dollars. This sail was interesting because it was an annual race between Bill and his longtime friend Peter Flanigan. James Panero and Roger Kimball were also there. Peter won the race each year but Bill never gave up hope. As we sat there on Peter's boat—lunch on the winner's boat—Bill mentioned that he had one H. Upmann left. Knowing that I occasionally smoked, since I had given him cigars on a number of occasions, Bill looked in my direction and said, "Larry, how would you like to smoke it?" "Bill, I couldn't possibly," to which he replied slyly, "Well, if you don't, then someone else will." I promptly agreed to smoke it, and having located it on Bill's boat, *Patito*, I came back with the box that had a Post-it note with "1940s" written on it. The cigar was spectacular.

As the months wore on and the expense of living in New York ate into the grant, I again faced existential questions about remaining in New York. Bill had the foundation release the remaining funds for my research work and no firm deadline was given for the report. I felt a responsibility to complete the project and also wanted to secure my position in New York for the long-term. Peter Gelb at Sony Classical offered me some consulting work, which extended my runway in New York.

The major moment for my development as an impresario in New York came when I reconnected with Martha Argerich, the greatest living pianist. She wanted to play a benefit concert in Los Angeles for the Santa Monica-based John Wayne Cancer Institute (today known as the John Wayne Cancer Foundation) which had saved her life with a cancer vaccine that was in clinical trials but never made it to market. I volunteered to produce the concert and convinced Argerich to move the concert to Carnegie Hall and to play her first major solo recital in twenty years. This was something the classical music audience had been waiting for, and I knew the concert would sell out immediately. I advised the John Wayne Cancer Institute to rent Carnegie Hall but this plan ran afoul of Carnegie Hall's management, which wanted to present what it also knew would be a legendary concert. To the uninitiated, when one rents Carnegie Hall, one can charge any price for tickets and basically run a gala in tandem with the event. If Carnegie Hall itself presents the concert, the tickets are priced according to other concerts it presents. My goal was to raise as much money as possible for cancer research, and this could only be accomplished by having the John Wayne Cancer Institute rent Carnegie Hall. Trying to rent Carnegie Hall was where we ran into roadblocks.

During this complicated period I attended the taping of the last episode of *Firing Line* on December 19, which was itself followed by the taping of a special episode of *Nightline* hosted by Ted Koppel. This was the first time I saw Bill become uncomfortable in a situation: The opening *Nightline* montage of Bill's career included his infamous duel with Gore Vidal from the 1968 Democratic National Convention. That debate was the one instance where Bill publicly let his temper get the better of him and where Vidal, a truly vindictive adversary, got under Bill's skin. That moment, captured on film for posterity, blindsided Bill that day and one could see how his regret about it had lingered for decades. He looked at Koppel and said, "I thought that footage had been destroyed."

The back of my head can be seen in that episode of *Firing Line* like Forrest Gump. Two photographs with Bill on the *Firing Line* set that day are the only ones I have with him from our entire friendship.

**William F. Buckley, Jr. and the author at the filming
of the final episode of *Firing Line* on December
19, 1999. Courtesy of Lawrence Perelman.**

As I navigated the situation at Carnegie Hall, I went to Schuyler Chapin for counsel, since I knew that the City of New York technically owned Carnegie Hall. He said there was little he could do to help but would make some calls. A compromise was ultimately reached and I remained a producer of the concert and also produced a reception at Steinway Hall where we raised additional funds for cancer research.

In my box at Carnegie Hall that triumphant sold-out evening of March 25, 2000, sat my parents along with Bill and Pat Buckley, Schuyler Chapin, Peter Goodrich, and Daniell Revenaugh, who introduced me to Martha Argerich and remained a close advisor. Saul Zabar, who became a friend, was also my guest at the concert, and sponsored part of the post-concert reception at Steinway Hall with some of Argerich's gourmet favorites from his food emporium. Bill was wide-eyed and entranced by the entire performance. He had heard about this concert from me for some time and had seen the front-page article in *The New York Times* I had secured for the concert marking Argerich's historic return. The concert began with a standing ovation and Argerich alone on stage playing the piano in front of an audience for the first time in nearly two decades. The audience barely let Argerich leave the stage after the first half of the concert, knowing the second half would include other musicians. The end of the concert required the stagehands to remove the pianos so that the audience would leave.

Chapin headed over to Steinway Hall following the concert but I missed him by mere minutes since I had to tend to things backstage. I later learned that Chapin told Isaac Stern, the president of Carnegie Hall and the man responsible for saving the hall from the wrecking ball in the 1960s, that I was behind the concert. A few weeks later I spoke with Stern over the phone and he told me how impressed he was that the concert became a reality on three months' notice.

A few days later on March 28, 2000, I received this letter from Bill:

> Dear Larry:
>
> I'm not writing you by e-mail because you told me your system had broken down. But I'm writing as quickly as I can to tell you what a special evening that was and how delighted Pat and I were of course to hear that great great artist, but also to greet your mother and father whose pride in you is so manifest. And with good reason, the responsibility you took in

managing that extraordinary event. I was sorry we couldn't go to the reception, but that final encore did it—we got in at quarter to twelve and it wouldn't have been right to keep Jerry [the Buckleys' driver] from getting home after one o'clock. My guess is [Argerich] couldn't possibly have arrived sooner than an hour after that encore and I think it's wonderful she undertook to do so at all—again a tribute to you. Thank you so much for that wonderful favor.

With warm regards,
Wm. F. Buckley, Jr.

The New York Times reported on the concert the next day: "Carnegie Hall may not have offered anything quite like this since Vladimir Horowitz returned to the recital stage in 1965 after a dozen years of retirement. Here, on Saturday evening, was the electrifying Argentine pianist Martha Argerich in her first major solo appearance in 19 years."

Chapin wrote me as well ordaining me a New York impresario:

March 27, 2000

Dear Larry:

First, congratulations on your terrific success. Not since Vladimir Horowitz returned to Carnegie Hall in 1965 after a twelve year absence have I heard or seen such an audience response. She certainly is an incredible woman and a brilliant artist—I cannot wait for her next appearance.

From what you told me I gather there were a number of problems in connection with this event which, if I'm not mistaken, would constitute your "debut" as a concert manager. I've already heard from Carnegie Hall that they seem to have had a few difficulties with you, but the fact of the matter is that you pulled off the presentation. I'm certain this will not be your swan song in the music business.

Yours ever,
Schuyler G. Chapin

It was flattering that Chapin was on the receiving end of calls from Carnegie Hall about my goals as an impresario. I learned a lot from the experience along with the importance of compromise. The concert took place, funds were raised for cancer research and Martha Argerich's goals were reached to bring attention to the important work of the Institute.

It was clear to me that none of this ever would have transpired if not for Bill giving me the grant and bringing me back to New York to pursue my dreams.

After this flurry of activity, I returned to my research and reconnected with Chapin who now arranged a visit for me to Public School 86. My research materials piling up and my eagerness to complete the work continued to collide with the realities of remaining in New York. I aimed to complete the research and write the report by December 2000 and then begin a job in the performing arts early in the new year.

Bill invited me to go sailing with him on June 30, 2000:

Dear Larry:

I'm glad to hear from you…I'm putting down your name for Friday the 30th of June. If that's okay, plan to arrive in Stamford at 6:07, and tell Frances that morning that you will be there so that I can meet you. We'll sail overnight, and you can go home after lunch. Let me know if that's okay. And I look forward to hearing the [Beethoven Sonata Op.]110—you can play it on the Bösendorfer in the morning.

With warm regards,
Wm. F. Buckley, Jr.

The trip out to Wallacks Point was always a treat and had thrilling elements to it, with the house situated on the Long Island Sound, and it being a rare experience for me to leave the city, let alone visit Bill's actual home. In addition to playing Beethoven for him we played piano together in Bill's convoluted scheme where we each played one hand of a piano piece making for a messy jumble of notes. The first time I sailed with Bill was in the summer of 1999 on which occasion I met the architect Claudio Veliz who had been sailing with Bill for decades. This second sailing trip resulted in a lifelong friendship with James Panero. We were both recent college graduates, James from Dartmouth, and another protégé of Bill's. James had assisted Bill with his book *Spytime* a few years earlier and spent six weeks in Gstaad working on it. He had incredible stories about that experience, skiing with Bill, renowned guests at the dinner parties, as well as his time as a junior editor at *National Review*. We immediately hit it off and after dinner, when Bill turned into his quarters, we continued smoking our cigars and talking late into the night. The next morning as we drank the instant coffee and ate English muffins lathered up with butter and peanut butter (yes, butter and peanut butter!), Bill slyly alluded to the fact that we kept him up with some of our banter, but he was also very pleased that a friendship had formed between two of his protégés.

**William F. Buckley, Jr. practicing the piano
while crossing the Atlantic Ocean in 1975.
Courtesy of Christopher Buckley.**

In early fall of 2000, I set a deadline to complete the research and write the final report. It was approaching a year and a half since I moved back to New York and Bill never expressed any urgency about completing the project since he always saw it as complementing my other aspirations.

When I finally completed the research Bill invited me to lunch at the Carlyle Hotel on November 17, 2000. He had lunch at the Carlyle every three months with the legendary British-American writer Alistair Cooke, who became a household face and name as the longtime host of *Masterpiece Theatre* on PBS. Bill told me that this lunch marked the first time in their thirty-year friendship that Cooke couldn't make it. Instead, I got the lunch slot, and it couldn't get more Upper East Side than lunch at the Carlyle. The home of Bemelmans Bar, it is steeped in New York history. The pianist Bobby Short played in the bar for decades and was the Buckleys' friend, having played at their home on numerous occasions. To be seated with William F. Buckley, Jr., at a table was something special. This was my first one-on-one meal with him and we discussed everything from the research project to politics and the Argerich recital. I prepared him that I concluded that it was impossible to actually gauge "what the lack of art costs you." Nevertheless, my thesis was that if one ascribes a value to everything one learns in life, then never having listened to classical music would make one less aware of the greatness of humanity. Therefore, not listening to or learning about classical music made the average person less a part of the human experience.

I sensed that the door was closing on a chapter of our relationship with the completion of the research project. By this point it had been five years since we first met but, realistically, the friendship was still relatively new. What would happen when the research project was complete? I realized that except for playing some Beethoven for him after the sailing trip to Oyster Bay several months before our lunch, I hadn't played piano for him at all since our first meeting in 1995.

A thought popped into my mind, "Bill, it's been a long time since I *really* played piano for you. If you'd like me to play for you and some friends, please let me know and I'll do it anytime."

He didn't miss a beat, "What are you working on these days?"

I replied, "Beethoven's Op. 110 sonata."

He thought for a second, "I love that sonata. When could you have it ready?"

"Anytime, just let me know when you want it," I said.

There was *that* twinkle in his eye, "I'll let you know."

And with that we finished up our lunch, I handed him the final report, and we made our way out to Madison Avenue. The next day Bill sent an email asking if I would be available to play Beethoven's Op. 110 at the fortnightly dinner the very next Monday, November 20. I thought about it for a minute and took a chance, realizing that I had to do it, and replied that I would be ready. Although I gave up the idea of becoming a concert pianist, I didn't lose my ability to play at a high level. I went back to Steinway Hall and asked if I could practice over the weekend. They kindly invited me to do so, and for about five hours a day on Saturday and Sunday, I worked on the Op. 110 Beethoven sonata, the composer's penultimate sonata, also known as No. 31. To connoisseurs, it was simply known as the Op. 110, one of the Last Three Sonatas: Op. 109 (Sonata No. 30), Op. 110 (Sonata No. 31), and Op. 111 (Sonata No. 32). For those well versed in Thomas Mann: The Op. 110 figured prominently in *Doctor Faustus*. It is a work where Beethoven broke many conventions of sonata form and, having already been deaf for basically two decades, takes the pianist and listener on a journey to another world through a neo-baroque finale that is both ecclesiastical and cosmic.

I headed back to 73 East 73rd Street this time as the evening's entertainment and focus of attention. I had been a guest at several fortnightly dinners since the evening of my hazing with Peter Duchin in 1999. These dinners were always a magical experience, but this time was different. My responsibility was that of a performer and not a dinner guest, although dinner would follow. My focus was to perform "the Opus 110" for a group of notables and to give Bill some joy. Any performer has doubts about his abilities and questions himself before a performance. This is natural, and since performing wasn't my vocation these days, my nerves were definitely on edge and my eagerness to perform was front and center.

Bill invited me to arrive a half hour before the guests so I could warm up on the piano and acclimate. Walking through these now-familiar doors was still surreal. Bill greeted me at the door and took me to the piano. My parents sent some presents for Bill: Russian chocolates and a small Russian lacquer box with a fairytale painting. He was very touched by the gesture and most thankful. He fiddled with the lamps on the piano since I was using music and asked if I needed anything. I told him I just needed to warm up and he stood by to hear a few minutes of playing before disappearing.

The piano was a very old Bösendorfer, considered to be the only piano equal to a Steinway or even superior as a salon instrument. Bill often referred to it as "The Bösendorfer." Think of it as the Vienna Philharmonic of pianos having been the piano of the Austro-Hungarian Empire. I worked my way over the keyboard noting the places where it might require some attention and employed the skills imparted to me by Yakov to never complain about a piano and to find its strengths.

Guests began to arrive. I left the piano so that some mystery would surround the performance. It's not customary nor good form to practice as guests arrive. I also limited my interactions with guests to the bare minimum so that I could collect my thoughts and prepare for the performance. I saw Pat, who this time slyly asked, "How's the Argentinean?" referring to Martha Argerich. I said she was staying well and would be back in New York soon. The guests had all arrived and Bill asked everyone to make their way to the living room and choose a chair or couch. We all moved from the bright red of the library to the glowingly lit living room with over a dozen lamps and tiny lights that punctuated the ceiling, aiming at paintings throughout the vast space. I stood at the piano and Bill walked over with a yellow notepad and red pen and began to introduce me to the guests. I paraphrase:

> Some of you may know Larry Perelman from dinners here and as the young scholar who recently completed a research project for me trying to answer the question, "what does the lack of art cost you?" Today, he is here as a pianist having written to me some years ago, resulting in our friendship. He will tackle the Opus. 110 for us and we will accompany him on that journey. He will begin with a Chopin nocturne. Larry, over to you.

I was excitedly nervous and limited my remarks to thanking Bill and saying, "I hope you enjoy the Chopin nocturne in C minor and the Op. 110, which is one of the greatest works of music." Before I started to play, from the corner of the room came Pat Buckley's voice: "Bill married me for the piano." This was followed by bursts of laughter throughout the room. It turned out that the piano was from Pat's family and dated from 1927. Unbeknownst to me was that Pat made this quip at every piano recital at the maisonette.

At the end of the piano was a red armchair. It was Bill's place of honor. Most people are interested in watching the pianist's fingers. Bill preferred this position and watched the pianist's face so that he could see the player's emotions. Most of the time, though, Bill's eyes were closed, with his hand clenched to the piano as if summoning the music from the instrument. Occasionally, he would smile or exclaim, "Wow, did you hear that?!" Sometimes he would even grit his teeth when the difficulty of a passage was evident to all. He was a participant and cheerleader for the artist at work. It was a joyful experience to behold for both audience and artist. This was Bill literally being the impresario of the evening, having invited the artist and overseen all details of the performance, including choosing the work.

When I finished the last bars of the Op. 110 with a wash of sound that requires all of one's strength to muster, Bill stood up and clapped the loudest and smiled with the broadest of grins. He came up to me and said, "That was something!" I was overcome with feelings since this piece of music is powerful and draining, both physically and emotionally. Bill was quick to say to everyone that it was time to adjourn to the dining room. He was on a high, as was I. After greeting many of the guests more formally with the performance behind me, I saw that I was seated next to Bill. I sat down and the dinner commenced with twenty-four guests. Much of what happened after that is a blur, but it was celebratory and warm. Once again, there was a mock *Firing Line* but this time the focus wasn't on me, it was a current event. The editors would go at it about some national or foreign policy issue.

As the evening concluded with drinks in the living room, Bill thanked me again and I could tell that he was genuinely thrilled about the performance. This time I took the opportunity to propose an idea to Bill: "How about you pick any piece you want me to learn and I'll play it at a fortnightly dinner?"

"Larry, any piece? How about the Diabelli Variations?"

I retorted: "Within reason, Bill, so let's say any Beethoven sonata, except the *Hammerklavier* and I'm not a fan of the Diabelli."

He thought for a few seconds, "How about the *Tempest* sonata?"

"Deal!" And with that, I walked back out onto East 73rd Street with my friendship with Bill firmly linked to the performance of music. The research project complete, he noticed something in my playing that night that made him interested in hearing more. These recitals would continue for years to come and become the centerpiece of my life.

Not two weeks after my performance, I received the following letter:

Larry:

A small gesture to thank you for a wonderful half hour of music for enchanted editors.

W.F.B.
11/29/00

Enclosed was a $500 check. I called Bill and said, "I can't accept this check." "Larry, I expect to be paid for my writing and you will be paid for your playing." I decided not to offend him by sending it back. He also had a point that reflected his character. He did not take talent for granted. He recognized the hard work that went into preparing a piece like the Op. 110. This wasn't charity, it was remuneration and to be expected by an artist, but not by a friend. It taught me never to take people's work for granted, especially that of younger artists who often merely receive dinner in exchange for a performance at a gala. Bill was a writer and was paid for every word he put to paper. Writing was his talent and he knew its value. It was a reciprocal relationship and reciprocal value was ascribed to the talents of each individual. This was a very special quality of Bill's that is rare today.

In early December, my parents received the following letter from Bill:

December 5, 2000

Dear Mr. and Mrs. Perelman:

How wonderfully kind of you to send me those gifts, visual and edible, via your son Larry. He played brilliantly, the Beethoven sonata and the Chopin. He also made a great hit with all of the guests and editors. He is such a fine, gracious young man, a great tribute to you both.

With warm regards,
Wm. F. Buckley, Jr.

As the end of the year 2000 approached, I received the final letter from Bill related to my research project.

December 27, 2000

Dear Larry:

You have done a fine research project. I have read avidly the essay, and it is as much as the Historical Research Foundation could hope for, given the impalpability of the haunting question, What actually does good music do for you? You touch on many aspects of this and there are many discouraging signs. The so-called "Mozart effect" and the "keyboard effect" are nicely presented and analyzed, and there are interesting surprises which you have unearthed.

You are free to use the material in any way you want. I'm sure you will want to make a copy for Schuyler Chapin. And perhaps you can get the word out to educators that they can have copies of it—at their own expense. As I think you know, the Historical Research Foundation has no budget for getting the information out on the research it has sponsored. My congratulations to you and my warmest regards.

As always,
Wm. F. Buckley, Jr.

The finality of my research project was clear, but through my performance of Op. 110, Bill and I had just started our musical journey and with it our friendship would flourish over the next eight years as I learned lessons from the impresario himself.

Chapter 15

BACH, BEETHOVEN, AND COLUMBIA

After playing Beethoven's Op. 110 for Bill, my recitals at the maisonette would take place at a rate of one every six or eight months. They were highlights of my year, and over time I even mustered the courage to ask Bill if I could invite a couple of friends to attend. I don't have exact dates for many of the recitals between 2001 and 2006, having lost many emails from that era when changing email addresses. Nevertheless, based on the repertoire, which I learned at Bill's request, there were at least a dozen recitals that included Bach's C minor partita, E minor partita, and A minor English Suite, as well as the remaining two of three last Beethoven sonatas Op. 109 (No. 30) and Op. 111 (No. 32), and his magnum opus, the Diabelli Variations. There were some other pieces as well by Bach, Chopin, Liszt, and Schubert. I also repeated some (especially Bach's E minor partita) and relearned pieces by Chopin and Schubert which I played in my youth. Bill's favorite composers by and far were Bach and Beethoven. Beyond that there were some visits to Wallacks Point and a concert there during the holiday season in 2006.

In a pamphlet "Memories of Evenings with the Buckleys at 73 East 73rd," Linda Bridges described what a private recital at the maisonette was like:

> Two or three times a year, Bill would get the idea of a musical evening. Most of us, if we develop an enthusiasm for a musician, buy his or her CDs and watch for notices of public performances. Bill would do those things too—but he would then invite the artist to play for him and, very important, for his guests. Bill often described himself as an evangelist—"We come upon wonderful things," he once wrote. "And it is hell to keep such things to oneself." He was writing specifically there about Red Wing peanut butter, but the same sentiment applies to musicians. Rosalyn Tureck or Fernando Valenti or Ignat Solzhenitsyn would surely have been willing to play for Bill alone. But Bill would not have enjoyed it a fraction as much as having the artist play for him and Pat and two dozen of their friends.

One fortnightly dinner, I played the C minor partita. This partita became an obsession of mine after I discovered Argerich's recording. The work was permanently etched in my mind when she played it at Carnegie Hall in March 2000. It has a *capriccio* movement, which in some ways foreshadows the Ragtime era and lands squarely next to Scott Joplin. It's as though Bach got to this movement and the spinning in his mind took on a different level of intensity. Every person should listen to it and try to comprehend the level of genius it took to compose this. Bach is systemic but within the system there's also a flexibility that bends time and space. Within all of this is the *capriccio*. It is daunting to think that it is but one star in the universe of his compositions.

Richard Brookhiser recounted that night in his book, *Right Time, Right Place*:

> Bill's regulars were Bruce Levingston and Larry Perelman, Bruce a concert pianist, Larry a serious student who had decided to serve mammon, but who kept the music in his fingers as an earnest amateur. Larry cut himself no slack; he played (not all on one night, to be sure) Beethoven's last three sonatas, in which modernism, postmodernism, jazz, and opera all jostle almost insanely. But the performance I remember best, because of Bill, was of the c-minor partita by Bach. After the tumultuous capriccio that ends it, Bill said that there was a passage in that movement that had made his old friend Fernando Valenti say, despite being an unbeliever, that he believed in God whenever he played it. Bill asked Larry to play the movement again, and said he would stand by the piano and indicate the passage when it came. The left hand went boom-chk, boom-chk, boom-chk, like [Dick] Wellstood playing Fats Waller, and the piece spun like equations or galaxies. Bill raised his arms over his head and grinned; love and work had delivered beauty, as promised. I doubt if politics gave him that sort of solace; it was his job.

To Brookhiser's point, politics probably never gave him that solace. I'll never forget an occasion where Bill said to me that "politics is my vocation, not my avocation." When one looks at the record of Bill's life, one will find that music dominated his spare time, the limited non-vocational time he had. We know he aspired to be a musician and gave it up as a teenager realizing he didn't have the talent. Nevertheless, he found ways to bring music—or "good music" as he would say—to his friends, readers and viewers. His friendship with Rosalyn Tureck, the foremost Bach interpreter to precede and follow Glenn Gould, was long-lasting and included multiple appearances on *Firing Line*, both at the studio and at the maisonette, where she not only spoke about the state of the artform but performed Bach. She also played private recitals at the maisonette and Wallacks Point, some of which were released as commercial recordings.

Rosalyn Tureck and William F. Buckley, Jr. on location at the maisonette for an episode of *Firing Line* on June 7, 1989. Courtesy of the Hoover Institution.

The episode filmed at the maisonette was dated June 7, 1989, and titled "The Fight for Bach." It sees Bill sitting in his red armchair in the living room interviewing Tureck who had just released a new recording of the Goldberg Variations. The entire discussion is about Bach's place in society and whether it is diminishing or increasing. At the end of the episode Tureck plays Variations 28 and 29 on the Bösendorfer with poise and grandeur. Bill is holding the armchair with all his might peaking over to get a glimpse of Tureck's whirling fingers on the Bösendorfer's ivory and ebony keys. As she approaches the conclusion the camera lands right on her smiling heroic face as a euphoric "bravo" erupts off camera. There's an audience of Bill and the production crew. Bill claps joyously and though one can't see his face, it's clear that the enthusiasm is akin to a die-hard baseball fan watching a slugger hit a home run for the win.

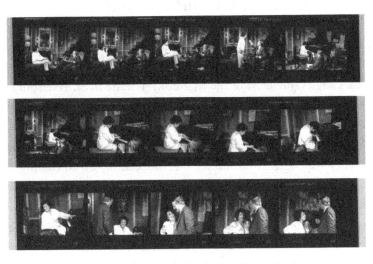

Rosalyn Tureck performing on the Bösendorfer at the maisonette for an episode of *Firing Line* on June 7, 1989. Courtesy of the Hoover Institution.

That's what it was like to play for Bill. He was the ultimate fan of both composer and pianist. He once said to me of
a Bach prelude I played with a bit too much rubato and peddle,
"Chopin would have been happy with that performance." He
was there with you all the way through. Anytime I felt some
nervousness at the keyboard I would look at Bill in his mesmerized state knowing the joy he was experiencing. And he was giving me the opportunity to continue playing the piano. At this
point in my career, as I approached age thirty in 2006, I was far
from a professional concert pianist. Gone were the days of practicing hours and hours. However, each time a Buckley recital
approached I would focus on completing a sonata or partita. It
was cathartic for me, as I worked in the business of music, to
have this friendship where making music was paramount. Each
time I completed a work and performed it, I couldn't wait to ask
Bill, "What piece should I learn for you next?"

I graduated from my impresario role with Argerich to working
as a public relations and strategic advisor to the great conductors
Gianandrea Noseda and Valery Gergiev and to the Salzburg Festival. Gergiev, the head of the Mariinsky Theatre in St. Petersburg,
has since fallen out of favor in the West due to his proximity
to Putin, but twenty years ago he was in his prime. I recall a
fortnightly dinner where I was seated at Pat's table along with
Henry Kissinger. After dinner I introduced myself to Kissinger
and mentioned that I advised Gergiev, to which he replied, "I
love that guy." It was my experiences with Bill that prepared me
to work with great artists and institutions. His trust in me gave
me the confidence to speak with anyone in the world. That
same evening, which must have been 2003, the cracks in the
conservative movement over the Iraq War burst into the open
when, during the mock *Firing Line*, there were three opposing

views taken on how the Bush administration should continue in Iraq. I clearly recall Kissinger standing up that night and saying, "America must be ruthless with its security." It was a *Doctor Strangelove* moment, if there ever was one. The proximity to these statements and observing the machinations of the power center was fascinating.

Bill was directly responsible for my ascent in my field. Returning to New York was only possible with the grant and the confidence it gave me. From there I was on my own to make my way but stood firmly on the bedrock he placed under my feet in the rough and tumble city of New York. I continued to live very modestly with my choice of industry far from remunerating me at the level of investment banking. I made a calculated decision to pursue a profession to perpetuate the art form of "good music." Of course, reality would set in between the aspirational moments of being at the maisonette and returning to my tiny third-floor walk-up on 84th and West End Avenue. Nevertheless, I always remained optimistic and was a free market entrepreneur who looked at the glass half full. This confidence given to me by Bill made the next step in my life a reality.

Ever since I first stepped foot on the Columbia University campus in 1994, I knew that I belonged. I took classes at Columbia University while at the Manhattan School of Music, including Russian literature and political science. Those experiences made me realize how much I enjoyed a liberal arts college, hence hastening my move back to Minnesota to attend Macalester College. The Columbia campus was absolutely magical and I yearned to one day attend Columbia Business School. In 2001, I mustered the courage to ask Bill for a recommendation and he wrote one. He provided me with a copy:

To Whom It May Concern:

Columbia Business School

I have interviewed, seen, [sic] worked with hundreds of young people in my career as editor and journalist. Lawrence Perelman is one of the two or three [sic] outstanding young men I have ever met. His credential and biography tell you everything you need by way of c.v. I add the following. He introduced himself to me a half dozen years ago as a student interested in piano and music. He engaged my attention and I brought him into our house where he performed for the editors of my magazine at our fortnightly dinner. He mingled with his seniors, showing great social skills and affability. We stayed in touch and a few years later, graduated now from college, he performed again for the editors and found himself in charge of Carnegie Hall on a blessed evening with the great Martha Argerich consenting to perform under his direction.

He has decided to apply for business school and understandably inclines to Columbia, because of its reputation and its location at the heart of the musical capital of this hemisphere. He will excel in anything he does, and I most heartily commend him to your attention, knowing that your investment will be profusely repaid.

Yours faithfully,
Wm. F. Buckley, Jr.

That first attempt at Columbia Business School failed since my GMAT score wasn't the greatest. I never enjoyed standardized tests and didn't prepare. Knowing what Bill wrote gave me an amazing amount of confidence to redouble my efforts in the future. I decided to give myself another few years to build up my resume and then take another crack at the GMAT with more preparation. The intervening years exceeded my wildest dreams and I traveled to Europe countless times advising some of the greatest artists and institutions in the world. I applied to Columbia Business School again and this time I was accepted.

When Bill wrote my second recommendation to Columbia he sent it to me in a sealed envelope to submit with my application. Here's his cover letter accompanying the sealed envelope:

October 5, 2004

Dear Larry: I have filled out the form for Columbia, and I enclose it in a sealed envelope, which came in with your CV. What you have accomplished is really impressive, and I have no doubt of your success. Thanks a million for the Schubert [CD], which I will swoon over for days to come.

With warm regards,
Wm. F. Buckley, Jr.

R. Glenn Hubbard, then the dean of Columbia Business School and a well-known conservative who had served as chairman of the Council of Economist Advisors under President George W. Bush, once told me that "it's not every day that an applicant has a recommendation from William F. Buckley, Jr." Well, it didn't seem to work the first time, but it did the second

time! I found myself entering Columbia in August 2006, but
not before undertaking an Everest of music: Beethoven's Last
Three Sonatas. Bill joined me on that extraordinary journey.

Chapter 16

THE LAST THREE SONATAS

Life can't be all bad when for ten dollars you can buy all the Beethoven sonatas and listen to them for ten years.

—WILLIAM F. BUCKLEY, JR.

There's a tradition amongst some entering graduate school students to undertake a major challenge like hiking the Appalachian Trail before embarking on a new chapter of study and life. After my acceptance to Columbia Business School, I gave notice to my firm and took on some consulting clients. This gave me extra time to return to the piano and dedicate myself to learning, in a few months' time, Beethoven's Sonatas Op. 109 (No. 30) and Op. 111 (No. 32). With Bill's favorite Op. 110 already completed, this would round out the composer's Last Three Sonatas. I set the goal of my thirtieth birthday on February 25, 2006, to perform all three. Peter Goodrich at Steinway & Sons helped me to secure Steinway Hall for the concert on March 2, the nearest available date to my birthday. Steinway Hall seated about a hundred people, but

I wanted to keep it to around fifty. This way it would remain a salon recital and the smaller the audience, the less likely for me to become too nervous and realize the craziness of what I was undertaking.

I waited until late evening on February 18 to email invitations since I was still learning the Op. 111 and had doubts about going through with it. I finally bit the bullet and pressed send:

> Dear Friends,
>
> I turn 30 later this month and have decided to play a piano recital for you.
>
> I may live to regret this idea but it seems like a good one at the moment.
>
> The recital will not take place on my actual birthday but on Thursday, March 2 at Steinway Hall in NYC.
>
> I will begin promptly at 7:00PM.
>
> What will I play? Beethoven's last three sonatas: Op. 109, 110 and 111 a.k.a. Nos. 30, 31 and 32.
>
> Will I have a page-turner? Yes, a very skilled one.
>
> This informal recital will last about 90 minutes.
>
> The details...
>
> Larry Perelman's 30th Birthday Recital
>
> Thursday, March 2, 2006
>
> 7:00PM

The Last Three Beethoven Sonatas

Steinway Hall

109 West 57th Street
(between 6th and 7th Ave.)

RSVP to me.

Bill was among the first to RSVP the next morning:

> Larry, how TERRIBLY exciting!!! Do they have
> at Steinway Hall facilities for wine and pastries
> or whatever at the end of a concert? I would
> be glad to finance this if okay by you. Advise.
> What a THING you are taking on!!! Be sure to
> invite Chip McGrath, who so much enjoyed
> it when you did the 2nd Partita [c-minor
> partita]. XXB

I was incredibly moved by Bill's offer to pay for a reception. I wrote back concurring that the undertaking was "TERRIBLY exciting with an emphasis on TERRIBLE. Hahaha...I hope I make it through all of them [the sonatas]." I confirmed that Steinway Hall had a caterer but wasn't sure how to accept his extraordinary offer and continued, "It is too generous. I am VERY, VERY touched. Beyond words, actually. How would I reciprocate? A performance of the Hammerklavier? The complete first book of the well-tempered clavier? Please advise."

Bill's reply moved me even more, " Larry, I am very proud of you and wish to express that pride. What kind of money are we talking about? How many are you inviting!! XXB" I accepted his generous offer and confirmed that I would have between fifty and sixty guests and the budget for something like this would be $1,500 to $1,750. Bill wrote back simply, "Larry: I'll give you a check for two grand, and if it costs more, well—don't worry about it, and I won't. XXB."

I took the opportunity to reiterate my gratitude and clearly convey to Bill what he meant to me:

> Bill,
>
> I really don't know what to say…
>
> I want you to know that after my parents you have been the most important person in my life. I mean this sincerely and with all of my heart.
>
> It's going to be a great night and I can't wait to see you there!!
>
> Let me know if you need ANYTHING from me. I mean it.
>
> > Warmest,
> > Larry
>
> P.S. Do you mind if I thank you in the program? Please advise.

Bill's final reply that day motivated me more than ever to deliver a stellar performance, "Larry, your note is more than any reward you could possibly give. Should I send the check? To which address??? XXB." His reaction to my note meant to me that he truly understood how important he was to me. This was essential to me.

Bill's generosity has been mentioned in other books, including Brookhiser's *Right Time, Right Place*. My experiences and observations add to those testaments of generosity and how voluntary, selfless and anonymous they were. In Bill's final two years of life our interactions became more frequent and his requests for performances multiplied. In a particularly raw and unvarnished interview with Charlie Rose in 2005, around the time of Bill's eightieth birthday, Bill conveyed to Rose that he was ready to die. He seemed dejected and even turned down the hypothetical pill that Rose offered that could make him twenty years younger and allow him to relive everything. Bill was emphatic: "Absolutely not."

The Bill in this interview is very different from the one I saw during musical encounters. There was something about music that gave him life, or the willingness to live. I'm not saying he would otherwise not have lived for another two years but the magic of music, only to be surpassed by his religious faith, may have played a role. In that interview he even pronounces that he's not thinking about "suicide," which would be antithetical to his faith, but given the darkness of the conversation and his pointedness with respect to being ready to die one couldn't help but think it.

This is why looking at our correspondence from this period is all the more intriguing. On the day of the recital, March 2, Bill confirms he will bring $2,000 in cash and responds to my question about whether I can mention him as the underwriter of the reception, "I'll bring cash DO NOT mention my patronage, but thanks for thinking to do so. Am SO nervus and excited for you! XXB." I included Bill in the list of "special thanks" but did not mention anything about the reception.

I was very nervous about the recital but even more excited. It had been a decade since I had given up the piano as a career, but here I was sitting at Steinway Hall ready to play the Last Three

Sonatas. My friends were assembled but sadly my parents had decided not to fly out for it. My parents' reasoning, going back to childhood, was that they could potentially jinx the recital. This was ridiculous superstition but very much their modus operandi. In addition to Bill, those in attendance represented my life in New York, including the composer and violist Ljova Zhurbin, who served as my page-turner; James Panero; David Bell; and *60 Minutes* correspondent Bob Simon, who also had a real love of classical music. Alas, Peter Goodrich, without whom the evening would never have taken place, couldn't attend due to a prior commitment.

To play one of the last three Beethoven sonatas is a challenge, and in my invitation I had called the recital "informal" in order to hedge against any lapses or major mistakes. However, the insecurities that may have plagued me going into the recital subsided as it began. Playing at Steinway Hall was like playing at home. This was a quasi-religious experience and I had known of this place since I traveled here on the synagogue trip fifteen years prior. Instead of recollecting here I will let Bill's words describe the evening in the following pages. The recital went very well and I had a few minutes to chat with Bill after finishing the Op. 111. He discreetly gave me a folded stack of hundred-dollar bills amounting to 2,000 dollars. I thought we would have a chance to speak more at the reception, but he slipped out quickly; he was the master of the stealth exit. The day after the recital I received the following note from him: "Larry, your evening was one of the most gratifying I have ever experienced. Deepest thanks, XXB." I tried to call him that afternoon and left a message on his machine. He replied, "Sorry I missed your call. I am here most of the day tomorrow. Thanks for your kind words. XXB."

I wrote back:

Bill,

I am extremely touched by your words and thrilled that the evening left this impression. I cannot thank you enough for being a part of it and for your generosity. The reception was a success and it gave a chance for all to get to know one another. Thank you so much for making it a reality. I'm sorry I missed seeing you off last night but I was still in a daze. I called earlier but couldn't reach you. I'd like to speak with you and will try you at home tomorrow.

I'd also like to reiterate that my playing has survived over my years in nyc in large part due to your encouragement.

Thank you for everything and I look forward to speaking with you tomorrow and playing for you again on March 20.

Warmest,
Larry

We spoke the next day, March 4, to firm up details about my next performance at the fortnightly dinner on March 20 where I would play the Op. 110 and Op. 111 sonatas.

On March 5, I received an email from Bill containing the following article:

By William F. Buckley, Jr.

Notes on the Passing Scene

I have said about myself, and repeat it here, that living in New York, or having easy access to it, can reproachfully grate on you. There are those so inattentive to the resources of the city that we live as if at the Grand Canyon with the shutters always closed.

I haven't counted, but there must be 100 musical events every day in NYC, and if you add dance and visual exhibits, make that 500. I write of a minor affair on March 2nd, the kind of thing that can just happen in Manhattan, in this case under unusual auspices because the impresario was celebrating his own 30th birthday. The modest, affable, gifted man had come to town eight or ten years ago from Minnesota, attracted to a career as a performing pianist. But he yielded (perforce?) to the usual stresses, and is now about to enter business school.

Tonight's was a special celebration: Lawrence Perelman sitting at a resplendent Steinway grand piano in one of the most alluring rooms in New York. Behind the hall, where musicians and their friends can gather in modest numbers, are the rooms that display the precious (a Steinway grand costs $90,000) artifacts of ivory, wood, and metal that give forth music. The invitations for tonight, sent out only a week or so earlier, were addressed to a few dozen friends, invited to hear him play.

Five minutes after 7 p.m. he hadn't come on stage, and we felt suspense building. Overhead at Steinway Hall is a great crystal chandelier. Behind the piano are slabs of gray-black marble, framing the large arched window with the plush, relaxing drapery at either side. Above the recess is a balcony with copper-colored railing. Right, at floor level, is the desk of the hall's manager, in finely burnished wood, behind it two yellow sofas, matching two others on the left end. Two grand oil paintings hang on either side. On the left is Franz Liszt, playing to feminine admirers—though maybe it is Anton Rubinstein who is seated at the piano, performing in a salon somewhere in Europe a century and a half ago. On the other side it's Wagner, depicted writing something on manuscript paper, with flying Valkyries overhead.

The suspense was for two reasons, the first, what sometimes sets in at the theater just before the curtains actually part. Tonight there was also suspense brought on by the sheer audacity: Larry Perelman had elected to celebrate his birthday by playing three of the most demanding pieces of piano music extant, the last three sonatas of Ludwig van Beethoven. Those who have pursued aural pleasure will have heard Sonatas 30, 31, and 32, but only those who are ambitious, and preternaturally skilled, will undertake to perform one of them, let alone all three at one sitting.

Five minutes later, the dark-haired celebrant walked into the room, dressed in a black suit and sweater, tieless, accompanied by a friend who would turn the pages. He smiled at his guests, made a brief comment on what lay ahead, and sat down to the Vivace of Opus 109.

Twenty minutes later he paused, accepted the applause, and then brought his hands down on the Moderato cantabile of Opus 110. His head was all but immobile even in the stormiest passages. He played through the sublimity of Beethoven's last piano works with precision and devotion. One quickly knew the artist's mastery of his material, noted the nimbleness of fingers that had Olympian challenges to perform, and wondered at his faculty for absenting his own personality so that we had only the music to hear in the gilt of the chamber. Seventy minutes later, he reached the quiet ending chords of 111, leaving the audience rapt by the music, and by the undertaking. Think, furtively, of the young matador confronting six bulls in one afternoon, the actor undertaking serially all of Shakespeare's tragedies on successive days—the painter, on Day One, starting in on the whole of the blank ceiling of a church.

It would be neat to finish here by saying that this kind of thing happens all the time in New York. But not quite. New York is a great, endless stage for star players in music and dance and drama, but the kind of thing Larry Perelman did cannot be regularly scheduled because dazzling acts of artistic adventure happen only in very special moments—like tonight's. A young man, at 30, decides to take on a music mountain, to dazzle others and himself by laying down one more wreath for the master, before settling down to learn accounting.

—WFB

I was in shock, flabbergasted, and my eyes welled up. I had only competed in a dozen or so piano competitions in my teens and never gave a concert that was reviewed by anyone. Here was a testament by William F. Buckley, Jr., on my playing. It was the greatest gift I had ever received about my playing. It was momentous for me to think he actually wrote it.

I vividly recall walking in SoHo with my mom and receiving his email with his article. I immediately called him. He was at his desk at Wallacks Point. I conveyed to him how astonished I was that he would write this and thanked him profusely. Mom hadn't spoken with Bill since briefly seeing him at his eightieth birthday dinner the year before. I thought how often this moment would happen and asked Bill to hold on for a second so she could speak with him. Mom thanked him for everything he had done for me over the years especially for keeping my playing alive.

A few minutes later I received the following email from Bill, "Larry, SO pleased you liked it and I thank you for your generosity of expression. What a treat to talk for a minute to your proud mother!! XXB." Unbeknownst to me it was Bill's intention to publish his piece in *National Review*. On March 9, he emailed me, "I hope you will enjoy the piece about you in the mag—but you can't see it until it is published! Friday. XXB." The article he sent me as a gift was published in the March 27, 2006, issue of *National Review*. I was speechless.

* * *

Not long after I visited my friend Steve Sherman's studio; he is one of New York's great photographers having photographed countless artists from Bernstein to Pavarotti. He had taken pictures of my Steinway Hall recital as a gift and we were reviewing the proofs. I was excited that there would be some images of Bill at Steinway Hall but couldn't find a single one with him—he was just too swift. The old CIA operative had slipped right by and disappeared into the night.

* * *

Performances were coming in quick succession now, and after the thirtieth birthday recital we already had a recital scheduled for a fortnightly dinner on March 20. Bill specifically wanted Beethoven's last sonata, Op. 111, which he cryptically called "the one eleven." I warmed up with the Op. 110 and then played the Op. 111. By this point arriving and performing at 73 East 73rd Street had become a regular part of my life. The thing that was changing with the passage of time was that both Bill and Pat were becoming more fragile, especially Pat. She was often with a cane these days. There was one evening where she simply said, "All my friends are dead." Someone started a slight chuckle at her statement before stopping, for with Pat one wasn't sure if she was being sarcastic or sardonic. In this case, it was the latter. There was another evening when Bill had invited me to a fortnightly where pianist Bruce Levingston played a run-through recital in advance of his performance at Alice Tully Hall. Levingston prefaced a piece by Bach mentioning that he was slightly nervous to play it since Rosalyn Tureck had also played Bach on the Bösendorfer. A voice could be heard from the far corner of the room, it was Pat announcing, "Bruce, don't worry, Rosalyn is safely interred." Everyone cracked up, yet the focus on death was becoming more present than distant.

After playing "the one eleven," I again asked Bill to choose a piece for me to tackle. He said, "How about the E minor partita. It's my favorite." It was as though he had already chosen it long before I asked. He would simply refer to it as "The E minor." I agreed and took on the task of learning this, the sixth and final partita by J.S. Bach. I wrote to him the next day thanking him for "the glorious evening." I continued:

> It really does feel like a family event when I play at the fortnightly dinners. The familiar faces, the warmth of spirit...it's all so special to me. I cannot thank you and Pat enough for your hospitality and graciousness over the years.... The E minor Partita is next on the list and I better get to work soon, for b-school is not going to help my technique!

These last few weeks have been surreal in so many ways and I will forever be proud and humbled by your beautiful words in NR, as well as your generosity on so many levels. Thank you. Good luck to you on the next book (how far along are you?) and let's definitely speak soon to plan some informal two hand sight-reading! XX-Larry.

Bill replied, "Larry, you embarrass me by writing before I could to express the gratitude for your display of skills, and reciprocate your affectionate friendship. XXB."

I next performed on September 19, 2006, a few weeks into Columba Business School, and managed to pull off completing "the E minor" in parallel with the rigors of the first semester. There was a statistics midterm the next day and escaping that preparation for an evening with Bill and Bach was wonderful. I recall that John O'Sullivan invited me to get a drink after the dinner and I couldn't say no to a former editor of *National Review*. This was my childhood dream continuing to come alive, where I was given the opportunity to interact with the mightiest political minds. I probably should have passed on the drink since that statistics midterm was one for the ash heap of history.

A few days later I received a letter from Bill: "Larry, last night was profoundly wonderful. And you don't let us down even when you are NOT at the piano. I enclose a modest honorarium. XXB." Enclosed was a $500 check. It had been years since Bill had sent a check and I knew not to call or try to return it. Nevertheless, it foreshadowed things to come as he approached his eighty-first birthday in November.

I played "the E minor" one more time that fall for Bill's birthday. He truly adored the piece and wanted to hear it as much as possible. I was in the haze of business school, where the first year has the highest burn rate for brain cells, but with an upright Steinway in my apartment arranged by Peter Goodrich, I was able to continue practicing and keep my music alive. Looking back now it's remarkable that I kept playing at a high level. It was entirely because of Bill and the tradition we had established in 2000. I always found time for Bill because I was convinced, and still am, that I wouldn't have made it *back* to and made it *in* New York without him. He provided the impetus and was the impresario through his selections and by hosting the recitals. He also lived vicariously not having been able to attain this level of playing earlier in life. When Bill asked me to learn something, come hell or high water, I was going to learn it.

In mid-December, I was in Minnesota visiting my parents during winter break. I heard from Linda Bridges that Bill hadn't been well and that it was serious. I emailed him on December 15 to see how he was doing but was discreet not knowing who knew what about his health. He wrote to me the next day, "Larry just out of curiosity, do you carry the VI partita [the E minor] in your fingers, or do you have to sweat up a storm to renew it?? XXB." I was reassured that he wrote back and decided to be less coy, "Hi Bill, I carry it in my fingers. Let me know when you need it. I spoke with Linda via email and she advised that you've been under the weather. I hope you're feeling much better. Warmest, Larry." Bill wrote back immediately, "have been in hospital with pneumonia but will catch you up. XXB." I wrote back that my parents and I sent him our best wishes for a swift recovery. The next morning Bill's reply came, "YES! I need YOU to perform JSB [J.S. Bach] on Dec 29. Everything is on hold waiting to hear from you. ((there will be a slight fee)). XXB." I wasn't planning on returning to New York until January but how could I not come back to perform the E minor for Bill? Moreover, he was recovering from pneumonia! There was no question I would do it and never told him I flew back for a couple of days to play it. This would be my gift to him after everything he had done for me. I spent the next two weeks working on the E minor partita in Minnesota.

With December 29 fast approaching, the following email arrived from Bill on December 27:

HERE ARE SOME UPDATES CONCERNING THE MUSIC AT WALLACKS POINT ON FRIDAY, DECEMBER 29, 2006

–Pat believes that to schedule guest-arrival for 5 PM is too early. I think she is correct. Accordingly, we expect our guests to arrive by 6 PM.

–Jerry will leave from the office (215 Lexington) at exactly 5 PM. He can transport 8 people. Larry Perelman gets priority, but he is arriving by train at 3:51 to fiddle with the piano.

–Jerry transports, southbound, transports Brookhisers (2), Nordlinger, Ramsey, Dick

Coming on their own are Peter Flanigan and guest, Sam Tanenhaus, Sam Vaughan, Roger Kimball (2), Larry Gilgore (2), Fr. Fitzpatrick.

–I assume that we will have greeted each other perfervidly, have had time for an eggnog or whatever, permitting me to introduce Larry Perelman at 7 PM.

–Larry will play one of the most gorgeous pieces of music ever written, Bach's VI (E Minor) Partita. He will play on a Bösendorfer which was selected for me twenty years ago by Rosalyn Tureck, who twice performed on it, pronouncing it as fine a piano as she ever played.

–Larry Perelman is familiar to our guests as the young man, a student of [business] at Columbia, who last fall decided to celebrate his 30th birthday by giving a concert at Steinway Hall: No less, the three last sonatas of Beethoven. He performed the E Minor Partita at 73rd Street in November, as a birthday present for WFB. The piece is monstrously difficult to play, and is profoundly rewarding. The music will take us to 7:45.

–Drinks and dinner will be served. Peter Flanigan will give a speech about moderate Republicanism. WFB will open his mouth for anyone who wants to look at pneumonia in the raw. Sam Tanenhaus will explain why he gives such hospitable coverage to recent turkeys.

–The diaspora will begin approx 9 PM. There is no need to note the train schedule since Jerry can handle everyone who is returning to New York. Other guests have made their own arrangements.

This would mark my third or fourth visit to Wallacks Point. I had sailed with Bill on two or three occasions and then there was dinner a few days after September 11. I had never played a recital at Wallacks Point just some casual sight reading with Bill. He would ask pianists to sight read but in a sly way. We weren't sight reading four-hand scores but two-hand scores. He would sit on the right side of the bench and play the treble section with his right hand. The guest would then sit on the left side of the bench and find it very uncomfortable to sight read the bass section since the positioning wasn't ideal for one's left hand. Bill would chuckle when we did this and say, "Is everything OK?" It was his way of having the upper hand on the piano with the advantage intentional and the outcome giving him immense pleasure as the superior player. I did this with Bill on a few occasions and they lasted for mere minutes.

Performing the E minor partita was always an intense experience and this was even more so the case since I didn't know what to expect when arriving at Wallacks Point. I was pleasantly surprised that, although slightly weakened, Bill was in pretty good form. He had a big grin and commiserated with everyone during the arrival cocktails. I particularly recall Pat being in the best mood I'd ever encountered and perhaps this was due to the fact that she was relaxed at home at Wallacks Point instead of being in the city. After cocktails, Bill introduced me, even though by now we were acquainted after many years of recitals, and I sat down to play. As Bill noted in his invitation, this was a much newer Bösendorfer and the sound was crystalline. I navigated the piano and the warmth and lushness surrounded me for this occasion. I performed with the thought that this could very well be the last time I played for Bill. This became the case with each of the forthcoming performances. As I finished the performance I heard some murmuring but focused on completing the final movement. Since no one tried to stop me I thought to remain steadfast and sail to the end. When the applause began I looked around and Bill was gone. The pneumonia had drained him and he had to excuse himself before supper. Pat remained and although Bill had retired upstairs, we all toasted him and Pat, wishing good things and good health in 2007.

Chapter 17

"VIVA VOCE"

My focus at the start of 2007 was Columbia, and my major reason for aspiring to attend business school was to build a cable channel for the performing arts. This was a goal I had shared with Bill many times since I became obsessed with the idea. Specifically, I was convinced since the Argerich concert in 2000 that Carnegie Hall could become a powerhouse media brand and performing arts channel. I believed that leveraging the power of that brand would make distribution through cable companies much easier than starting a channel with a generic name. I had asked for guidance on this idea from Bill along with other mentors like David Bell, Brian Beazer, Peter Goodrich, and most recently Leo Hindery, an executive in residence at Columbia. Leo was a cable industry warrior and legend. He ran TCI cable and oversaw its merger with AT&T broadband into one of the largest cable companies in America. He then founded the YES network, the Yankees' sports network. He knew a thing or two about leveraging powerful brands. Upon entering Columbia I had one goal: Meet Leo. I did, and we hit it off. Leo offered to incubate my concept at his private equity firm during the winter semester. Soon I found myself at the Chrysler Building with an office and access to Leo and his colleagues.

During this time I had mentioned to Bill the idea of inviting R. Glenn Hubbard, dean of Columbia Business School, to a fortnightly dinner. Given everyone's schedules it took months, and we finally settled on Monday, April 9. This time things were starkly different. On March 9, Bill wrote to me:

> Larry, there is this problem, Pat is immobile, and needs one of the maids with her, so I am left with one maid and one butler, so I decided to initiate the evening as we had it once before. Namely, up to 24 guests to HEAR YOU PLAY and to get drinks and hors d'oeuvres, but for dinner, maximum of 11. Would those [Columbia Business School friends David Disi and Michael Livanos] mind just coming for the music and drinks??? XXB

> Did you have in mind the Partita and #111? Is there a problem of too long, or could you do the partita without all the repeats? How long is the Beethoven, about 20 minutes? Advise. XXB

I expressed my concern about Pat then asked that he clarify *which* partita, since he didn't say. "The partita is E minor (number 6). However, would you like me to relearn the C minor [partita]? I can do that instead. The plan was to do the partita without repeats which in the case of the E minor would be about 20 minutes or so. As for the Beethoven...it's about 20 to 24 minutes." Bill took the repeats question very seriously and this would often come up when we were planning the recitals. "You are amazing!" Bill continued, "Let's do the E minor, which is my favorite, and then the Beethoven. Thinking in terms of 40–45 minutes. And let me know if your guests can make it. XXB."

On March 28, Linda Bridges and I were finalizing details since the guest of honor would be Dean Hubbard. Linda had recently taken to co-hosting these dinners. She wrote, "Mainly owing to Pat's unwellness, we're doing it as a one-table event, so probably there will be no one but the editors, you, and the Hubbards. But stay tuned." Bill and I had confirmed that the program would run 50 minutes and feature the E minor and "the 111." Linda chastised me for not confirming the exact timing of the recital with her since the staff at 73 East 73rd thought it was going to be shorter. Bill and I were back-channeling about the program and not copying Linda. I apologized and said that going forward I would re-confirm all timings with her.

Bill and I emailed again on April 4, and I confirmed that two business school friends would attend for drinks and the recital. One of my friends, David Disi, was an Iraq War veteran and Bill was eager to meet him. "By all means," Bill wrote, "Drinks, concert—but no dinner!!! XXB Can't wait…. Are you figuring about 35 minutes for the partita and 30 for the Beethoven? GAWD, what you take on!!!! XXB." I confirmed that each work would run about twenty-five minutes and asked if he really wanted all of the repeats in the Bach. His reply was classic, "On the Bach, could we repeat the last two??? XXB." He was referring to the last two movements, which I think he wanted repeated to give him just a bit more of the Bach he so fervently loved.

The fact that this recital happened at all was due to Bill's resolve. It wasn't known to me, and possibly to most guests, that Pat was in the hospital being prepped for surgery the next day. Bill's expressions during recitals were always focused on the joy the music gave him and the crusades undertaken by the performer. This recital was no different, with Bill sitting at the end of the piano, hand grasped, looking over to the piano and laser focused on the performance. To think that all of this was going on while Pat was awaiting surgery and that he went forward with hosting this recital is unfathomable except for the fact that he needed the musical catharsis. I understand from other writings that Bill couldn't confront Pat being in the hospital and the risks associated with the surgery. This could explain deflecting the reality with the sublimity of the music he loved.

During the dinner, Bill stepped away from the table to take a call. He later mentioned it was a call from the hospital. The dinner went on and poor Dean Hubbard, who thought he was being welcomed into a genteel environment with the editors of *National Review*, was actually grilled by them. He smiled through it all and was a complete sport, but I think he might have had second thoughts accepting the invitation if he knew that after the recital Bill, Larry Kudlow, Rich Lowry, and others, would put him on the *Firing Line* with questions about President George W. Bush's monetary and non-monetary policies, including the Iraq War.

At the end of the evening I said to Bill, "As you know, it's your responsibility to pick the next piece for me to learn." Without missing a beat Bill said, "*the* Diabelli" and I shot back "I hate *the* Diabelli, what about *the* Liszt Sonata?" Bill quickly added, "I *hate* the Liszt Sonata." For the first time we were at a standstill on repertoire choices.

The next day I wrote Bill a thank you for the evening, sending prayers for Pat's continued recovery, and mentioning that Hubbard both had a wonderful time and that his sixteen-year old son had tried to tackle "the 111." Bill responded:

> Oh Larry, you embarrass me by speaking first. You gave us such a divine evening, and your playing moves forward together with your presence, a man of manners, a cosmopolitan, and an artist.... Pat will be in the hospital another week, and bedridden who knows how many weeks. But I may call on you just the same....
> I liked Mr. Hubbard, and am impressed that ANYONE should tackle the 111! XXB

Pat went into surgery that day and a few days later slipped into a coma from which she would never wake. She passed away on April 15, 2007, from an infection related to the surgery.

I can't imagine the grief that Bill felt. Christopher Buckley wrote a raw yet heartfelt book, *Losing Mum and Pup*, in which he delves deeply into those final days. His recollections at time become extremely personal, but what does one expect? I'm blessed that both of my parents are still living and that they have been married for fifty-six years. That's two years shy of what Bill and Pat celebrated. To live life together for so many decades, the relationship and existence becomes symbiotic; as mentioned earlier, they shared the same nickname, Ducky. I had only known them for a sliver of their fifty-six years together, but at this point it wasn't an insignificant sliver—eight years. I never knew Pat as well as Bill, but her presence was constant and over time I saw an affectionate side she didn't often display. She realized that my friendship with Bill was based on Bill's favorite avocation, music. Up until that night in April 2007, she was always present at the recitals, and I think she enjoyed them even though she was not as inclined to classical music as Bill. Nevertheless, the piano in the maisonette came from her side of the family, without which there never would have been these recitals on an imposing, imperial piano fit for this majestic room on Park Avenue ruled by this iconic socialite.

Deciding when to write to Bill was difficult, but I did so two days later, expressing my entire family's condolences and saying that I was there for him anytime. I didn't expect to hear from him for weeks or even months when, on April 20, Bill wrote, "What would you think of doing the Bach/Beethoven at Wallacks Point for just a few people on Sunday evening?? XXB." I immediately replied saying that I would be there. Bill wrote, "Larry, you are a saint. Please stand by, and I'll see if I can put it together. XXB." That same day he wrote:

> April 22. Mass at 5.
>
> Guests arrive at 5:45.
>
> Larry should take the 3:34 Express arriving Stamford at 4:21. If there is no one there to meet him, he should take a taxi to Wallacks Point
>
> Drinks at 5:45, concert at 6:30
>
> Expected (invited) Kimballs (2), Fitzpatrick(1), Danny, Mr. and Mrs. Edgerton, Mrs. Tom Hume, Trish Bozell, Brent Bozell.
>
> Julian will serve hors d'oeuvres after the music.

I will need hotel rooms at local Stamford hotel
for Perelman and Bozell.

The next day, another note from Bill, "Larry, you are a saint
to be so obliging. But we'll have to postpone the concert—
three or four critical guests simply couldn't make it on Sunday.
Thanks for being so agreeable. XXB."

The next time I saw Bill was at Pat's memorial at the Metropolitan Museum of Art for which she had raised millions upon
millions over the years. I went with James Panero. This event on
May 14 was illustrious to say the least and matched the woman
it was memorializing. A Who's Who was in attendance at the
Temple of Dendur. Caviar, served. Veuve Clicquot, served. Peanut butter on Ritz crackers with bacon bits, served. One of Pat's
favorite drinks, the bull shot, served. I had never had a bull shot
until that day or since. Here, the bull shot was served in a large
wine glass. The recipe calls for Campbell's beef bouillon, vodka,
and Worcestershire sauce. It had an air of a society function but
was a memorial. I saw Bill and he seemed fine at the beginning.
I came up to him and we embraced. By the end of the memorial,
after Henry Kissinger and Christopher and others had spoken,
I saw Bill again. He was completely broken and inconsolable. It
was difficult to bear witness.

The next day I wrote to Bill and expressed again how moving the memorial was and added "Please know that I'm here for
you. I'll be back in New York in early June and we should plan
on some Bach. I've begun work on Diabelli." The last line was
important since I had put off learning the Diabelli Variations
for Bill for many years. More on that later. Bill replied:

> Larry, it was lovely to see you there, and I hope
> you will be within reach for me always....

Larry, bright thought. Would you like to come to Stamford on Thursday and play either the Beethoven or the Bach before dinner? We'd get you back PROMISE not too late. If the answer is Yes, I will suggest a train that gets here about 6—not earlier, because I can't interrupt my working day...I'm thinking out loud. There is a 5:23 that gets here at 6:07. I have to worry about the piano being tuned I'll see what can be done. XXB

In the midst of all of the emotion from the memorial, Bill was inviting me to Wallacks Point to play for him. In hindsight it is extraordinarily touching to think that he was in need of music and thought of me. I had just flown to Minnesota to visit my family and offered to fly back for the day on Thursday. Not surprisingly, Bill offered to pay for the flight back, which I said wouldn't be necessary, but after some additional back and forth we agreed to wait until my return to New York in June.

Deep down I knew that there were fewer days ahead with Bill than behind us. However, I always remained optimistic, and letting Bill know that more music was being learned for him was a way to keep him focused on the future. An incredible quality of Bill's was looking forward, not back. In the wake of Pat's death he focused on his work and continued writing his columns. There was a freshness to his writing and almost an impatience with having to wait to write the next column. He mentioned in that reply that "I can't interrupt my working day...." That was Bill. Those who knew him would marvel at his discipline with time and efficiency. It continued in some form until his final breath.

On June 5, I wrote Bill that I was back in New York, imply-
ing that I could come to Wallacks Point to play for him. "Well,
grand to know you are back," he wrote. "Let me think up of
a proper celebration and see if it works for you. XXB." A few
days later when checking my mail, I found a letter. It had been
some time since he corresponded by mail and the envelope was
the familiar white one with the light blue italicized "William
F. Buckley, Jr." on the upper-left-hand corner. The letter was
date-stamped June 8, 2007. My mind flashed back to the first
letter I had received from him nearly thirteen years ago in
1994. The difference this time, and from other letters he sent
over the years, was that my name and address weren't typed,
but in red pen and barely legible. Bill himself had written out
my name and address. It was a miracle the post office was able
to discern it. As I opened the envelope, I noticed the paper was
yellowish and the letterhead was not embossed but typed. The
letterhead wasn't from *National Review* as it had been in the
past but hand-typed and from the Wallacks Point address. It
seemed like this letter was from a manual typewriter and from
Bill's own hand. My heart dropped as I read it:

> Dear Larry:
>
> What is enclosed is very simply a gift. It is, to
> be sure, an appreciation of your attainments,
> but hardly conceived as a reward for them—
> such rewards to [sic] received from other
> quarters. It is, simply, a gesture of appreciation
> and admiration, from a friend who greatly
> esteems you. XXB

My eyes welled up with tears. Attached to the letter with a paper clip was a $10,000 personal check from Bill. I wasn't sure how to react. Was this a farewell? My first instinct was to call Bill. We had last been in touch a few days ago. I called my parents to share with them Bill's latest gesture. They were shocked and we were all concerned for Bill, hoping that he wouldn't let go of life. It saddened me that I wasn't able to deliver on Bill's wish to have me come play Bach and Beethoven days after Pat's memorial in May. I wanted to bring some light into Bill's darkness and I wasn't able to do so.

I called him but the phone just rang and rang. A few hours later, I tried again. I was walking on the Columbia campus. He answered the phone.

"Bill, it's Larry."

"Hey, buddy," Bill said.

I continued, "I received your letter and check. I'm not sure what to say. Your words and generosity are beyond words." I knew better than to say that I would return the check. There was something going on here that was bigger than me. He might be settling his affairs as he anticipated the inevitable whenever it came. "Bill, I've said this before but I want you to know you are, along with my parents, part of the group of most consequential people in my life. Thank you for your friendship and everything you have done for me over the years. I'm here for you, just let me know when you want me to come and play for you. I'm working on the Diabelli Variations and want to play them for you when they're ready."

Bill was touched and replied in his swift and efficient manner, "Larry, thank you so much for your words. I cherish our friendship and I can't wait to hear you play again. We'll get together soon."

We said goodbye and all things considered he sounded like the Bill I always knew. Bill seemed to be thriving on email and fine on the phone but in reality there were other things boiling beneath the surface.

About a week later I learned from Roger Kimball that Bill wasn't well. I emailed Bill and heard nothing. I then emailed Linda Bridges, who replied, "No, he's not well at all. In fact, he's in hospital." This resulted from forgetting to take some medication and dehydration. He would remain in the hospital for several weeks with things looking bleak from time to time. Christopher sent out medical bulletins keeping friends apprised of Bill's progress. In mid-July Bill replied to one of my emails saying to "Check back in a fortnight." He sent a personal update to friends on July 30 saying he was improving each day and had just completed a book about his friendship with Barry Goldwater. However, he wasn't yet up for visitors: "Healthwise; My strange disease continues substantially to incapacitate me. I can't walk without a cane or the use of somebody's stout pair of shoulders, but Christo detects day by day improvement. The question is whether day by day will happen before surrender time." It closed with, "Remember me in your prayers. And those of you who do not pray will understand my plight. I truly love my friends, and one day will be able to say so viva voce."

I knew the days were fleeting. I often thought I would never see Bill again. Nevertheless, I redoubled my efforts on the Diabelli so if and when Bill pulled through and again opened his doors, I would be ready with the ultimate gift for him, a performance of "the Diabelli."

Chapter 18

DINNERSTEIN AND THE GOLDBERGS

On September 14, 2007, I saw Bill for the first time since Pat's memorial in May. Roger Kimball picked me up from the train station in Stamford and we drove to Wallacks Point where Bill awaited us. We had lunch at Jimmy's Seaside Tavern, a local haunt that Bill had frequented for many years with Christopher and friends. My recollection of Bill was of a worn-down, unshaven version of himself, but still very much himself. Towards the end of his life he began to use an oxygen machine but I don't recall one during this visit. He was definitely using a cane but if anything he resembled an old sailor with the sailing cap, which was omnipresent when he was anywhere near a dock.

It was wonderful to be with Bill again and to see that he was moving about and able to have visitors. He reached into his bag and pulled out two CDs he was excited to share with us. He slid them across the table to Roger and me proclaiming, "This is the greatest recording of the Goldberg Variations I have heard in my entire life." The pianist was Simone Dinnerstein. I knew her name and had heard a few tracks of this recording when her management was shopping it around to record labels. My impression of those tracks was a playing of warmth and clarity. Not having heard the entire thirty-two variations didn't allow me to argue Bill's point in any meaningful way. Then again, why argue? Bill had been friends with Rosalyn Tureck, one of the foremost Bach interpreters of the twentieth century, and Fernando Valenti, one of the most acclaimed harpsichordists of the same era. Music may have been Bill's avocation, but one could almost say he discerned music on an expert level and could easily have been a music critic. Bill gave us the CDs as gifts and asked us for our impressions.

As I looked at Bill, I couldn't help having my inner impresario jump at the chance to do something for him. On a whim I said, "Bill, how would you like Simone to play the Goldberg Variations for you?" Bill stared intently at me, "You can do that?!" I explained that I could contact her manager and make the pitch. He was extremely excited and said to proceed.

We returned to Wallacks Point where I played some of the Diabelli for Bill and Roger. The Diabelli was still a work in process, but Bill was overjoyed to know that he had won out and that I was learning them. It was bittersweet to be back at the piano in front of Bill. I felt for him as he mourned the loss of Pat, and if there was any way to bring him joy, then I would serve as that friend until the end.

As we left, Bill took us into his study and offered me some copies of his books. His study was a converted garage; he needed an epic amount of space. It was in some respects the conservative movement's Sistine Chapel. Lined with hundreds of books (including multiple copies of the fifty-four books he had written to date), the study was the ultimate work space, consisting of desks and tables strewn with papers, manuscripts, computers, typewriters, and assorted gadgetry from decades of curiosity spanning his Renaissance-man worlds, including those of sailing, music, and religion.

En route home I called Simone Dinnerstein's manager and got her assistant. I explained who Bill was by suggesting the assistant "Google" him. I then proceeded by explaining that Bill was mesmerized by Dinnerstein's playing, and we would like to invite her to play the Goldberg Variations for him. An hour later I got a call from Dinnerstein's manager, Tanja Dorn, who impressed me by already having spoken with the pianist. As fate would have it, Dinnerstein knew well who Bill was, having listened to a recording of Rosalyn Tureck playing Bach at Bill's house. This recording was close to her heart; she had listened to it while giving birth to her son.

I wrote to Bill:

> I spoke with Simone Dinnerstein's manager at IMG Artists. It turns out that Simone knows the Tureck recording that was made in your home. She would be honored to play for you and your friends. She makes her Wigmore Hall debut with the Goldbergs on October 21 and could conceivably play them for you around October 14. I'm not sure if this suits your schedule at all. Other options are definitely available. Please let me know your thoughts...

Bill was ecstatic, writing back, "You are SOMETHING!!!!!! But tell me...what would she expect from me in the way of...

compensation? As you know, we don't have fee schedule for those Mondays which you have made so golden. But first, did you listen to the recording? Do you share my enthusiasm? Is Monday Oct. 15 okay? XXB." The idea that I could make this a reality for Bill was of paramount importance to me. My life took its shape from being taught early on that anyone was reachable. That paid off in meeting Bill and now it would be fitting if I could repay him in a small way by bringing Dinnerstein and "the Goldbergs," as he called the variations, to him.

I was very impressed with the recording that Bill had given me and replied that it "was quite amazing. A very fresh reading of the work. I will listen again because there are so many compelling ideas. Thanks for the recording!" I continued, "As for compensation…I explained to her manager that there wouldn't be any compensation. Therefore, it should all be clear. If October 15 definitely works for you, then it should work for her. Please let me know." Lastly, I asked him, "would you see this happening in Stamford or New York?" "Larry, you are truly amazing!!!" Bill wrote. "Think this would be best in nyc. But if Ms. Dinnerstein doesn't care which, could we hold that open?? XXB."

It was amusing to me that Bill was so amazed this could happen. I met him, one of the busiest people in America, by writing him a letter. How hard could it be to make a pitch to a manager? This is the level of confidence that I had, and it was because *he* had made me believe that if you write or call someone with a succinct point, it's possible to meet just about anyone. "You're too kind, Bill. It's just a phone call that makes things happen, not to mention the fact that YOU are the admirer. I bet that either would be fine with her but I'll check with the manager regarding preferences." Since October 14 landed on a Sunday, I asked if Dinnerstein was available on Monday, October 15. She was, and soon she would be performing the Goldberg Variations at 73 East 73rd Street.

Bill was known for writing columns on subjects that consumed him, such as when he wrote a column about my research project and then proceeded to dedicate an episode of *Firing Line* to the topic. Therefore, it wasn't a surprise when Bill sent me his "latest musical thought" on September 25 to be published in *Gramophone*:

For Gramophone Magazine

I had ten brothers and sisters and music was a staple. My father enjoyed the kind of music he heard as a young man living in Mexico. He knew nothing about serious music except that it was serious, and so his instructions to our teachers were to expose us to: serious music.

There were two conduits for this, one a huge (Capehart) record player provisioned, the other, five pianos. The player was organized by [Penelope] a weepy lesbian high brow. She was in charge of teaching her four pupils the magic of it all, to which end, once every day, lights out, doors shut, and we heard one hour of music. We hoped this afternoon's would be Bach because Penelop would then surely weep, and her effort to conceal her emotion was a fine distraction and an opening for whatever inclinations the three girls and their brother (I was 11) had for Schadenfreude. If Penelope didn't suffer after listening to Bach—why else would she weep?—then we were having our way back at her for sitting us down one entire hour in the afternoon when, outside, the autumn leaves were brightening the grass, and the water in the pool was hardening into plate glass. I don't remember if the moment was communal, but it came there, at all four of us, hitting each rock-hard. Maybe in the second year, perhaps the third. But at some point we were bewitched by the music.

Simultaneously we were at work on the piano, under the instruction of another woman. She was a disciplinarian, like Penelope, but all love and laughter. I decided solemnly that I would become a piano virtuoso, along with my talented sister. I have read a lot of essays about great musicians but not many about musicians who failed to be great, perhaps because after a while it didn't seem to matter to the world at large whether you could yourself perform the Diabelli Variations, or had to settle down to hear them on a Capeheart. And then today, as the generations slid by, the record player was reduced to a few cubic inches, as portable as your paperback book, much more manageable than your lunky typewriter.

So, most of the children who set out to become virtuosi, failed to make it. That's easy. Not so the more interesting question, which asks about the communicability of the joy of music. Without giving the matter serious thought, I'd generalize that everybody enjoys music. By "everybody," I am excluding the here-and-there dumb creep (I have known two) who will not notice the Oratorio played at their own funeral. These are gentry intensely to be pitied, and every means of rescuing them from their malignancy must be taken. A Penelope hired, another schoolteacher gravely commissioned, vacation trips planned to musical events, jazz concerts encouraged, even scheduled.

Remember that the overwhelming majority will catch on, finding rhythmic and melodic pleasure in Mary Had a Little Lamb and, one day, sitting with pleasure through Parsifal. Many will fall by the wayside, but how to measure the gratitude of those who do not? You will get an impression of what you have awakened by looking at the photographs taken of young people lined up at dawn waiting for the ticket line to open, whether for the Beatles, or for the Budapest String Quartet.

It has to be the greatest free gift of modern times that we can have music pretty much whenever we like. And for all that you may think of the following as routine hyperbole. It was with no malice aforethought that I moved to this insufferable act of devotion. After hearing this CD two days ago I welcomed a lunch guest by telling him that I had just now had the single most striking musical experience of my life. To write such a statement causes one's fingers on the keyboard to be febrile, the mere thought of such a thing. I'm not certain I will ever run the risk of playing it again. But here it is: J.S. Bach's Goldberg Variations, performed by Simone Dinnerstein for Telarc International Corporation.

I worked with Linda Bridges to assemble the guest list and liaised with Simone Dinnerstein's manager. As the day approached, Simone asked to try the piano in advance of the recital. I coordinated with Bill and Linda to gain access to 73 East 73rd Street and escorted Dinnerstein and her technician to the maisonette. Walking into this vast dwelling without Bill present had an eerie quality, almost like being on a movie set, since the fortnightly dinners took place at night and our visit was during daytime. Dinnerstein was very gracious upon entering the lavish living room. Without even touching the Bösendorfer she understood that it was a very old instrument. I told her about my experiences playing on it, and as the technician began inspecting it, I stressed that this piano had history associated with it from Rosalyn Tureck to many others, both amateur and professional. Simone began the aria from the Goldbergs, and her tone made its way across the regal room. The technician listened along with Simone and me, and within five minutes Simone had decided the technician shouldn't touch the piano at all. She said the piano was perfect and she wouldn't put it through any voicing or adjustments. That was a respectful decision since having a technician do something to a nearly century-old instrument wouldn't help beyond a nominal amount, if at all. I think that Simone sensed the special nature of this instrument and decided to navigate it rather than initiate a mini-refurbishment with no time at all.

I kept Bill posted, "Simone is now playing through the Goldbergs at 73rd Street. She loves the piano. It sounds glorious. Simone will arrive to warm up around 5pm on Monday. Have a wonderful weekend and see you on Monday." "That is SUCH good news!!!!!" Bill wrote. "Am absolutely delighted. We don't have a proper guest room but she can be comfortable, I think, in my study. No, what I will do is turn my bedroom into a guest room for her! XXB How is she addressed, as Miss Dinnerstein? Can you give me just a half sentence on each of her guests? XB."

October 15, nearly one month to the day on which Bill shared the Dinnerstein Goldbergs with Roger and me in Stamford, there was Simone practicing on the Bösendorfer at the maisonette. This marked the first fortnightly dinner since my performance six months ago, a few days before Pat passed away. Bill stood by as Simone played and was trying to make sure the lamp didn't flash on and off. He was transfixed by the rehearsal before disappearing to give her privacy. The guests began arriving at 6:00 p.m.; drinks and hors d'oeuvres commenced. There was excitement in the air both for the performance to come and for being back at 73 East 73rd after six months of tribulation. It was a proud moment for Bill to be hosting a fortnightly dinner again, though it was tinged with Pat's absence. This room had seen decades of evenings, including at least three Goldberg Variations, one on piano by Rosalyn Tureck and two by harpsichordists Fernando Valenti and Gerald Ranck.

My recollection of this evening was that the audience was larger than normal. Although dinner would be limited to two tables, the concert was something that Bill reveled in, with dinner an afterthought. This was a night he couldn't wait to see arrive. After thirty minutes of cocktails and hors d'oeuvres and catching up amongst fortnightly dinner regulars happy to be reunited, everyone made their way to the living room to find a seat. The room was aglow and the anticipation of what was to come, the musical feat to take place, was intense. Once everyone was seated, Bill stood up with his notepad in hand. He cleared his throat and proceeded to introduce Simone and proclaim what he told friends and published in *Gramophone*, that the Dinnerstein Goldberg Variations were the finest he had ever heard. He then introduced Simone, who made her way to the piano almost floating across the room with her long hair enveloping her face, which had the slight smile yet seriousness about it akin to that of the Mona Lisa. The audience applauded and Simone said what an honor it was for her to be performing the work for Bill and his friends.

As Simone began to play, it was as though time had stopped. It was one of those evenings that one wanted to bottle and place in the cellar of one's memory. She took the Bösendorfer to heights it had only seen a few times in its eighty years of life and transported Bill, now eighty-one, to a desert island where he and the Goldbergs could exist for time immemorial. Looking back I am heartened to know that this evening happened. For one night, I played impresario for Bill, himself the ultimate impresario of the twentieth century. A lifetime of Bill's musical aspirations, along with the hundreds of musical evenings he and Pat had hosted over the decades, led to this night where we could all witness a private performance of the Goldbergs that in the mind of our host had given him more joy than any other performance of the work in his lifetime.

As Simone finished the last variation and took a pause before restating the aria, everyone in that room must have realized on some level that this would be the last evening of its kind at 73 East 73rd Street. That final recitation of the aria was as much a conclusion of the Goldbergs as it was a farewell to the Buckley fortnightly dinners and to a piece of history. She concluded the aria and there was a silence that felt like an eternity as all those in the room internalized the meaning of the evening and the power of what they had heard. We were all given this gift because William F. Buckley, Jr., was a part of our lives and fought tirelessly for his country during his entire life. This was our way to be with him in his final stretch home and worship together with him the music he so adored.

The applause began and Simone stood up from the piano with a smile of appreciation as Bill clapped and clapped with a joyousness we hadn't seen in some time. The applause went on and on finally fading as we all chatted about what we had witnessed. Cocktails resumed for another half hour until dinner was served to those who remained, with Simone sitting next to a smiling Bill who, as host, received the ultimate gift of her company.

Richard Brookhiser recounted the evening in *Right Time, Right Place*: "[Dinnerstein's] recording of the Goldberg Variations...caused a sensation: Some said she was as good as Glenn Gould, the eccentric titan who had made these pieces a pop hit; some said she was better; more important than better or worse, she was different, having squeezed out from Gould's shadow to reinterpret the variations in her own way." Brookhiser continued, "She brought out details I had never heard before; at moments she was so intimate one felt almost embarrassed to be listening in a room with other people. Bill's concert setup performed its usual tricks: One of the lightbulbs in the lamp on the piano sputtered and flashed at the fortes, causing Bill to lift himself up, so slowly now, out of his chair, to tap it."

The flashing lightbulbs and Bill's attempt to right them were as much a part of the Buckley experience as peanut butter on Ritz crackers with bacon bits on the tray of hors d'oeuvres. Nearly every time I played at Bill's, the lights would flicker and Bill would rise up and tap them quietly trying not to interfere with the pianistic ritual. How I miss those moments and the care he took as impresario. Perhaps that evening the flickering was Pat signaling that her spirit was still there with Bill and us.

Chapter 19

THE BUCKLEY VARIATIONS

A fter the Dinnerstein Goldberg recital, I flew to Minnesota for a week and committed myself to working on the Diabelli. This was one of the most complicated pieces I had ever set eyes on, and I knew it would require many hours of practice. Coupled with my business school studies and cable channel project, there would be little time for other activities. I saw the sands of time slipping away and understood that Bill had given me a goal of ASAP without overtly stating it. Even though Bill had mentioned the Diabelli as a piece he wanted me to learn on numerous occasions, it took some time for me to understand what he saw in it. I knew it was considered a masterpiece by pianists and musicologists, but my first impression of the piece as a teenager, when I heard it in recital, relegated it to the pile of pieces I would never want to hear again. Perhaps it was the performer, whom, unsurprisingly, I cannot recall, or more likely, my naivete that led to this decision. I just thought the Diabelli Variations were not for me. My preference was for the late Beethoven sonatas and the Liszt B minor sonata, which was something I *wanted* to learn with the limited practice time I had at my disposal. However, since Bill had stated his dislike of the Liszt, I knew I had to give in and honor his request, especially given his decline. Yakov Gelfand, my longtime piano teacher, always told me to learn pieces without listening to recordings, so I approached the Diabelli anew without any impressions at all. I bought the score in the summer of 2007 and started to make my way through it. I began to understand the work and Bill's desire to hear me play it as I invested hours and hours of practice to unearth the Diabelli's extraordinary musical message. When I visited Bill in September 2007, I had several of the variations under my belt and decided to share some of them with Bill to give him a glimpse of what might be. Learning the entire thirty-three variations would require much more dedication.

In 1819, Viennese publisher Anton Diabelli wrote to fifty composers asking them to compose a variation on his thirty-two-measure waltz. It takes one minute to play this ditty. Diabelli's plan was to sell the fifty variations in a bound book and thus immortalize his waltz alongside variations by Beethoven, Czerny, Schubert, an eight-year old Liszt, Wolfgang Amadeus Mozart's son, as well as a bevy of composers few would recognize today including Moscheles, Plachy, Kalkbrenner and Schoberlechner. Beethoven was the hold-out refusing to conform to Diabelli's plan.

What is undeniable is that Diabelli's thirty-two-measure theme wouldn't be remembered if not for Beethoven ultimately taking and transforming it thirty-three times; Beethoven's actual title, *33 Veränderungen über einen Walzer von Anton Diabelli Op. 120* (33 Variations on a Waltz by Anton Diabelli Op. 120). *Veränderungen* can mean *variations, transformations or changes* in the German, thus possibly broadening Beethoven's intent beyond the traditional musical variation form. Beethoven was deconstructing everything throughout his compositional life, especially as he became more and more isolated and locked in his mind as a result of his deafness. There isn't a consensus on exactly why Beethoven wrote thirty-three variations instead of joining the other composers. It took Beethoven four years to complete the composition and Diabelli published the grand work alongside another volume of variations by the other composers. Some musicologists theorize that Beethoven thought it beneath him to have a single variation alongside others. Thus, why not go over the top and compose thirty-three? By doing so he would outdo even himself—he had written thirty-two variations in C minor—as well as Bach, whose thirty-two Goldberg Variations were up until then the gold standard for variations. There's some credence to going head-to-head with Bach since Variation 31 of the Diabelli is a variation on Bach's Goldberg aria. Furthermore, Beethoven wrote multiple fugues in the Diabelli, a musical form championed by Bach and which Beethoven tackled repeatedly later in life.

I wrote to Bill after returning to New York on October 25, "I have practiced more in [the last week] than in the entire month preceding it…the Diabelli are coming along very nicely. This might sound crazy but I'd be willing to give its premiere before you leave for Florida [in December]. Is there any chance?" I continued,

> It's a monster of a piece and there's so much work. [Pianist and conductor] Hans von Bülow called it a microcosm of Beethoven's entire output. It surely seems to be the case. Thank you so much for focusing my attention on this masterpiece. Please advise how you'd like to

proceed with a performance. Ideally, I'd prefer two more weeks of practice…I hope all is well on all fronts. XX-LP.

The next morning came Bill's reply, "I am very free this weekend. Why not come, spend the night, and just practice it?? Advise. XXB."

On November 2, I took the train to Stamford where Bill picked me up from the station. I thought Bill's driving was shaky at best and as it turned out he shouldn't have been driving at all. Thankfully, we made it to Wallacks Point in one piece. I was told on a later visit that Bill was expressly forbidden from driving but remained committed to picking friends up from the station. Bill would come in and listen for hours as I practiced, working the kinks out of the Diabelli. One day I was digging through his pile of piano music and came upon a very old volume of music that was falling apart at the seams. The title of the book was *Diabelli Variations*. These Diabelli weren't Beethoven's, but sixteen of the fifty *other* composers commissioned by Diabelli. It seemed fateful that such a coincidence would happen during my visit. Bill was thrilled and called it "a find!" I sight-read through them one by one as he stood nearby expressing disbelief. Our favorite variation was by a composer whose name just slips off the tongue: Friedrich Wilhelm Michael Kalkbrenner. Bill and I had numerous meals that weekend and I asked for his counsel on my cable channel project, which was still in its nascent stages. He always encouraged my ambitions and for this I was profoundly thankful. He was enthusiastic about the possibility of a performing arts channel coming to fruition in America and said I had his wholehearted support.

"Thank you so much for a glorious weekend," I wrote to him upon returning to New York. "It was great fun not only to practice north of ten hours but to catch-up on all fronts with you. I can't remember the last time I ate so well over three successive days. The Diabelli really made serious progress and I'd venture to guess that they should be ready in a few weeks." I continued, "We were tentatively discussing late January or early February for the premiere. However, if you have a hankering for Diabelli please know that I'm eager to try them out.... Let's speak very soon and thanks again for a real treat this weekend. Warmest, Larry." Bill replied "It was wonderful to have your company and the sublime music. XXB."

The probability of seeing Bill before the end of 2007 slipped away. I wrote to him on December 23, "First of all, Merry Christmas to you and your family! Please excuse me for not being in touch. The last few weeks were consumed with end of semester activities, finals and projects. However, Diabelli hasn't suffered. He's better than ever. I will be in Minnesota for the next few weeks and then off to Japan for two weeks." I continued, "At some point we should discuss a date for the Diabelli. I could do it in early February. I do hope everything is well with you and that the Reagan book is coming along." Bill wrote, "Larry, Swell of you to write! And what a busy time you are having and I am surprised you can also fit in the Diabelli. I do not have with me here in Florida my editorial calendar but let's think in terms of the first fortnight in February. Is that okay? How exciting!!! XXXB."

The next month was a blur of activity and the jetlag after returning from vacation in Japan lasted almost as long as the two-week trip itself. As the jetlag-enhanced sun blazed on me in the chill of February, I wrote to Linda Bridges to check on a performance date. She was in Switzerland and conveyed that things were quite uncertain with Bill's schedule. He wasn't committing to too much entertaining and she would try to connect with him and then update me. We penciled in February 27 for the Diabelli to be performed at Wallacks Point. I heard nothing else and returned to my studies at Columbia as well as rekindling the Diabelli after two weeks away from the piano.

Then came Bill's invitation to play the Diabelli on February 19 which turned out to be the last gathering of his siblings. It was one of the most incredible days of our friendship and having my mom there as a part of it made it even more memorable. I couldn't wait to return to Wallacks Point to play the Diabelli again for Bill and friends on February 27. I wrote to Linda Bridges about preparing for the recital, "I'd love to arrive on the 26th and get some good practice in." Linda confirmed everything and closed with, "Bill promises that he'll ask you to do the Diabelli again in the city later in the season, so the rest of us can also hear it!"

Chapter 20

THE LAST SUPPER: FEBRUARY 26, 2008

As I awoke on February 26, I had a bit of a hangover after a night out celebrating my birthday with friends. I boarded the Metro-North from Grand Central Station to Stamford. Arriving late in the afternoon I found Julian, Bill's chef, waiting for me outside the station. He said that they were keeping Bill off the road. He added that Bill wasn't feeling well so he might not join me for dinner. We arrived at Wallacks Point around 6:00 p.m. I left my bags upstairs in the guest room, which used to be Christopher's bedroom, and approached the music room's doors with trepidation. I thought Bill might have ventured down for a meal to this room he so adored. I heard his oxygen machine roaring over the sounds of the evening news on the projection television. Opening the door, I saw Bill tinkering with the remote control, and a soda and a mixed drink with orange juice on the table nearby. The lunch with Bill and his siblings felt long ago even though it was just the previous week.

I gently placed my hand on Bill's shoulder and he looked up. In his trademark style, he uttered his classic, "Hey, buddy." I replied, "Hi Bill, it's great to be back." He immediately asked what I'd like to drink and I chose red wine. He rang the kitchen staff to bring the wine. Dinner had officially begun. I gave him a classic recording of Arthur Rubinstein playing Beethoven's Piano Concerto No. 4. I made myself comfortable on the couch next to Bill and we chatted about some odds and ends.

I reiterated to Bill what an honor it was for me to perform the Diabelli for him and his siblings last week, and he conveyed his delight and noted the impression that my "sweet" mother had made on the gathering. The first course arrived and it was simply red caviar and crème fraîche on toasted baguette. Bill inquired, "Would you like some vodka?" I replied in the affirmative. Bill then raised his shot glass and I mine, which followed with a clink and swift consumption of the perfectly chilled vodka. I found it incredible that here we were toasting with chilled vodka while watching news footage of the New York Philharmonic's visit to North Korea, one of the last vestiges of communism. Here we were, thirteen years after we first met, toasting to all good things with vodka and red caviar. It was very special and soon our glasses were refilled.

Bill opened the CD that I had brought and began to stand up to play it. Seeing him struggle I insisted that I do it. He let me go ahead. The recording began.

The second course arrived as the sounds of Beethoven's fourth piano concerto filled the room. This course consisted of wonderful fish, green beans, and some of the best mashed potatoes I've ever had; Julian knew how to use butter. Bill reminisced about concerts he had heard in the 1930s. Specifically, he mentioned hearing this, his "favorite" concerto, performed in London in 1938. He then turned to me and asked, "Do you think the harpsichord is today facing its greatest challenge as a concert instrument?" This was classic Bill and although far from being an authority on the harpsichord—he was one and called it the "Queen of Instruments"—I agreed with his observation. In front of us stood one of Bill's harpsichords, indeed one of his prized possessions.

Our conversation ranged from politics (such as North Korea and the primaries) to culture to mutual friends—James Panero, for one. I mentioned to Bill that, if not for him, James and I wouldn't be friends—and noted that many friendships were created as a result of his largesse. He remembered our sail to Oyster Bay eight years ago. I then told him that James and I had tried to live the "Buckley life" for a period of time. We defined the "Buckley life" as waking at 5:00 a.m. and heading to sleep at 10:00 p.m.—Bill's incredible regimen. I explained to Bill that, in order to make it work, James and I would call each other at 5:00 a.m. to make sure the other was awake. It lasted for barely two weeks. Bill roared with laughter.

Bill soon said, "We must talk about your performance. The issue of repeats in the Diabelli." Once again, here was Bill and the repeats! "What do you think?" Bill's question brought a smile to my face, and I said, "Bill, I'll repeat only the best variations, and it should clock in at about forty minutes." He then told me about the guests who would attend the concert the next day, asked for my preference whether to play before or after dinner (I always played before) and, finally, asked if I would like some cognac.

We finished up dessert, which for me consisted of a lemon tart and for Bill a plate of fresh watermelon. The lighting in the music room and throughout the house always created a hazy dream-like effect for me. Bill's Cavalier King Charles Spaniels were constantly begging and being shooed from the table. However, during desert Bill gave them both the chocolate chip cookies they obviously had been expecting. One played with the cookie on the floor between the two of us. Bill adored his dogs, and to my knowledge only had the regal breed Cavalier King Charles Spaniels throughout his adult life. The newest addition—"Isn't he a *champ*?" Bill said—was just five months old.

Just after eight o'clock, Bill said he was going to sleep. The oxygen machine wasn't portable so he removed his tubes and got up to walk. I assisted him for the next ten or fifteen minutes. Each step was a monumental struggle for him. The emphysema was relentless. He went public with his emphysema in a column in May 2006 after he had returned with the diagnosis from the Mayo Clinic. He wrote, "If you found yourself with emphysema, and you woke up emperor of the whole world, with absolute power in all matters of production and consumption, what would you do? That's simple, of course. Forbid smoking to everyone you care about." I followed Bill's lead as he walked, and there wasn't anyone else around. As he slowly made his way, I held on to him each step of the way. We reached the staircase where a mobile chair had been installed so he could ride up to the second floor. He sat down and the chair moved up the rail. I met him at the top of the staircase and helped him to his room.

One of the maids was now with us and together we seated Bill on the bed. This is where everything became foreign to me in terms of how I could help Bill. His breathing grew more pained as the maid tried to remove his belt which was keeping him from receiving adequate oxygen. He was struggling and struggling. Danny Merritt, thank goodness, arrived and helped to diffuse the situation. Bill regained his breath. For a split second I thought the worst since it seemed that Bill couldn't breathe.

Once I saw that Bill was comfortable, I excused myself and went back downstairs to finish my drink. I had a chance to speak with Danny who was helping to take care of Bill and the house. Danny was a childhood friend of Christopher's and from what I understand, he kept things in check for Bill. After we said goodnight, I walked around the living room a bit to let the history sink in. As I refilled my drink I noticed Campbell's soup bouillon next to the vodka; the bull shot was still a presence in the house. I had never had much of a chance during visits to Wallacks Point to see the pictures in the frames. There was Bill with Reagan, family pictures, and one of the Buckley family re-enacting the iconic Kennedy family football formation photo. These two incredible Catholic families were so similar yet couldn't have been more different on nearly every level. However, the families themselves were quintessentially American, with strong patriarchs who saw their respective spawns as capable of transforming their country, one from the Right, and one from the Left. Both patriarchs were correct.

Here I was, having just turned thirty-two, in the home of my friend, William F. Buckley, Jr., now eighty-two. How far we had travelled over the past thirteen years since we had first met. I didn't expect that he would die soon. I knew he wasn't well, but never in my life did I think that he had just hours of life left. Our dinner conversation was lucid and his memories solid. I went to sleep looking forward to again playing the Diabelli for Bill and his friends, most of whom had also become my friends over the years. As I closed my eyes I thought about our conversation that evening and the recital I was going to play the next day.

Chapter 21

PADRE NO MORE,
PADRE NO MORE!

I woke up from a deep sleep and looked at my BlackBerry. Ugh. 6:30 a.m. Footsteps in the hallway? It must be Bill going downstairs. I could still feel some of the hangover from my birthday now compounded by the vodka and other drinks consumed with Bill the previous night. I thought about getting up, but returned to my slumber. As I thought about the recital I was to play that day, February 27, 2007, I couldn't help but look at the glass as half full when it came to Bill and his maladies. As difficult as it was to watch him struggle to walk and breathe every few feet, it was still *our* Bill who was with us. And we were thankful to have him still.

I finally got up at 8:30 a.m., showered, threw on a pair of jeans, a T-shirt, and a sweater, and headed downstairs to the kitchen. This was to be my second performance of the Diabelli. When Bill would pronounce "The Diabelli" he would do so in a manner that could have been code for "You've got to be insane to attempt to play Beethoven's magnum opus, but good luck!"

A dozen friends were invited for this performance, with dinner to follow.

I walked into the kitchen and found Julian and the two maids in conversation; the Buckley staff was like family, having worked for the family for decades. When I said "Good morning" they laughed a bit, given that 9:00 a.m. was quite late in a house where Bill was now known to ring for breakfast at 4:00 a.m. or 5:00 a.m. I asked where Bill was, and Julian said he was out in the study. This corroborated that it was in fact Bill whom I had heard at 6:30. He was working on a book about the Reagan he knew. This was to be book number fifty-five!

After breakfast I walked to the living room, and once again encountered the Bösendorfer. I couldn't help but recall Pat saying, "Bill married me for the piano," back at the maisonette. The plush red carpeting warmly welcomed me into the room, and I sat down at the piano. I warmed up with some Bach and then *Widmung*, Liszt's transcription of the Schumann *Lied*. At about 9:30, after thirty minutes of practicing, I went up to the guestroom to change sweaters.

I thought about what a gorgeous day this was, and reflected that spring was on the way. As I donned my sweater I was startled to hear what soon would become a continuous sound of yearning pain. What *is* that? No one screams in this house. It was a female voice. I couldn't decipher the words and the sound was so out of place in this house. The hair on the back of my neck stood up and my skin went cold from the feeling of unease. Something wasn't right. Within seconds I thought that Bill must have fallen. I had been told that he had fallen a few times—he was losing his balance and as I saw the night before he was stubbornly reluctant to use a cane. But then I thought again and my mind darted toward the inconceivable. The expression on his face when he was short of breath last night starred at me in my mind's eye. I looked out the window and couldn't see anyone. That sound. That wailing. Where is it coming from? No. No. No. It can't be. No. No. Don't think about that. It's not possible. It's just not possible. "Larry, don't think about that."

I ran down the stairs in the direction of the wailing. As I entered the kitchen I encountered one of the maids. She was the source of the sound. I finally focused and began to reluctantly understand her. She looked directly in my eyes: "Señor... Señor...Padre no more, Padre no more!"

It still didn't sink in. I felt like I was in a Hemingway novel, "Padre no more. Padre no more." Over and over again. I immediately asked, "Where's Danny?" The maid showed me Danny's mobile number and I quickly dialed. No answer. "Where's Julian?" Earlier, Julian had told me that he would be heading to the store to buy some things for the dinner. "Julian there... Julian there..." she said, pointing in the direction of Bill's study.

I bolted out the door and ran the thirty yards to the study. The door was ajar and there was Bill. He was on the floor face down. His dogs were confusedly walking around him while the other maid stood crying. A shocked Julian was on the phone, and a fire siren could be heard approaching. Within a minute the fire engine arrived and the firemen made their way in with EMT gear. I stood outside the door and watched other medical personnel arrive.

I walked back and forth on the driveway near the study door. I was next to Julian when one of the EMTs came over and said that Bill had a DNR (Do Not Resuscitate) bracelet. There was a part of me that thought that maybe, just maybe, they were going to take him to the hospital and try to revive him.

Moments later the same EMT man came back and said, "Mr. Buckley has passed away."

I was shaken and couldn't comprehend what had happened. Bill was dead. He was gone. He was no more. How was this possible? One doesn't expect to be present at an unexpected death. To be present at any death is an emotional rollercoaster. However, when one has an expectation then one can be prepared. It's still difficult but you see it coming, Yet, when it isn't expected, even if the person is elderly, it comes as a complete shock. To hear of a death of a friend and process it is one thing. To be at his home, in the presence moments after he stopped breathing, is something that changes you. I didn't realize at that moment as I looked at Bill's body that he was really gone.

I looked at the American flag outside the study and at Long Island Sound. I thought about everything Bill had done for our country, and for my family, and the countless millions of people who waged battles against Communist regimes around the world.

The police arrived. It is a necessary formality in the case of any death at a residence. I walked into the house with one of the officers, and he asked me, "Did you know Mr. Buckley?"

I thought to myself, "Did I know Mr. Buckley?" Past tense. Why is he asking me this question in the past tense? The idea of death hadn't yet penetrated my mind. An hour ago, I would have said, "I know Mr. Buckley." This was the first person to ask me that question in this tense. From now on it was going to be, "I knew Mr. Buckley."

The police officer was an innocent bystander to the emotions I was experiencing. I looked at him with tears forming in my eyes and said, "He was one of my best friends." The officer replied, "I'm so sorry for your loss." With those words it became reality. My eyes welled up completely as I said, "Thank you," and ran up the stairs to the room where just four hours earlier I had awakened to the sound of Bill's footsteps. What was especially difficult to process was the fact that I had had dinner with Bill just the night before. It was sinking in, and I was sinking along with the feeling. I couldn't stop crying.

My BlackBerry began to vibrate. Text messages, emails, and phone calls began coming in. The news was out. Bill was still in his study, but everyone around the world was beginning to learn of the news. It was hard to talk to anybody at that moment as my phone rang. I had told a few friends that I was playing for Bill that evening but no one knew I was already at Wallacks Point.

Several hazy hours passed with endless phone calls coming into Wallacks Point. I spoke with Christopher for a minute to convey my condolences, but otherwise I didn't know what to do. Everyone in the house was functioning in a surreal state. The coroner finally arrived and someone said to me that it would be better to remain in the house than have that memory of Bill's body being moved seared in my mind. I prepared to return to New York and thought of calling a taxi to the train station in Stamford. Julian kindly offered to drive me, but before we left, I asked him, Danny, and the maids to gather in the living room. I had come to Wallacks Point to play for Bill and I said it was imperative for us to honor his memory with music that very afternoon. I proceeded to play the first prelude from the second book of Bach's *Well-Tempered Clavier*. This work in C major, the simplest of keys on the piano, managed to bring us together in our grief while also giving us a sense of salvation. I'll never forget the feeling of the tears raining down my cheeks as I finished the closing passage. As the sound disappeared, the five of us embraced and wept. This moment offered us catharsis and we would all deal with our grief in the days and weeks ahead. Our country would also face the reality that one of its greatest citizens had left us.

Chapter 22

SAYING FAREWELL

When I returned from Wallacks Point I called James Panero and asked if he wanted to get a drink. He agreed and, in turn, called Jamie Ewing to join us. Jamie was another protégé of Bill's and had, just like James, assisted Bill on a book in Gstaad. In Jamie's case the book was *Elvis in the Morning*, a novel about the American icon which to some seemed un-Buckley given the subject matter, but it showed Bil had a reverence for music beyond classical. Both James and Jamie witnessed first-hand Bill sitting at his desk with Bach's counterpoint swirling around him as he weaved together his thoughts and crafted his writings as if in a trance.

We met up at a bar in Gramercy and I recounted to them everything that had happened. I was in a daze having thought that I would be playing my recital for Bill and friends. We sat and shared stories of Bill and consoled one another as grief set in. James and Jamie co-owned *Patito* after having bought it from Bill and shared a love of sailing, which was never one of my hobbies. I was always the person standing cluelessly as Bill's first mate asked me to hand over a rope of some kind. We laughed and got emotional that night. We toasted Bill repeatedly and realized together how our lives would have been different had he not taken an interest in us as a mentor and perpetuated our ambitions through his largesse.

My parents were tremendously saddened by Bill's passing. Mom told me that she had expected it but didn't want to say anything to me as she sobbed on the ride back to Manhattan from Wallacks Point. As she often did since childhood, she wanted to shield me from unpleasantness. This was a trait that ran firmly through our family and probably many others. Why worry the children with mortality? I was a grown man, but my mom still wanted to protect me from the inevitable.

For about a week I wept each morning. It was both the loss of Bill and having dined with him the night before he died that weighed on me. I felt a responsibility to convey to people that he was himself that night. I wrote an article for *National Review* titled "The Last Supper with WFB," which was published on February 29 and is the basis of Chapter 20 of this book. Bill Kristol, then an op-ed columnist for *The New York Times*, wrote in his March 2, 2008, op-ed titled "The Indispensable Man":

> Bill died in his study early Wednesday morning [Feb. 27, 2008]. He had had dinner Tuesday night with Larry Perelman, who in a lovely piece on National Review's Web site described the evening.
>
> Perelman knew Bill because in 1994, at age 18, as an aspiring classical pianist living in Minnesota, he had written to thank him for fighting for freedom for Soviet Jews (Perelman's parents had fled the Soviet Union, that locus

classicus of immanentizers of the eschaton, in the 1970s). Perelman also had been moved by Buckley's columns on classical music. Perelman wanted to repay Bill by playing the piano for him. Bill invited Perelman to do so, and recitals at the Buckley home became a regular attraction for Bill and selected guests.

Perelman was scheduled to play Beethoven's "Diabelli" Variations Wednesday night, so he joined Bill for dinner the evening before to discuss the performance. They resolved the issue of how Perelman would handle the repeats in the Diabelli to their mutual satisfaction. They talked about music and politics and friends, to the accompaniment of a recording of Beethoven's Fourth Piano Concerto, Bill's favorite.

It's fitting that Bill's last evening was filled with music and graced by friendship, both of which gave him so much joy. It's fitting that he spent it with someone who had sought Bill out because of his uncompromising defense of freedom, the lodestar for his political and intellectual efforts. It was a fitting end to an admirable life.

My friendship with Bill was now immortalized and could stand as an example for others. It was an honor to know that millions of people would read this and learned that Bill was himself the night before he died.

On March 5, Linda Bridges sent a simple email notifying friends that Bill's memorial service would take place at

St. Patrick's Cathedral at 10:00 a.m. on April 4. It would be open to the public with seats reserved for family and friends. Dad instantly said he would fly to New York to pay his respects and attend the memorial with me. Mom preferred to stay in Minnesota since the experience of being at Wallacks Point in February was so overwhelming for her. My relationship with my dad has always been close but I sometimes imagine what it felt like to him that his son sought out mentors. It isn't that my dad couldn't offer me what I was looking for, he did, in more ways than he can imagine. The search for a mentor was driven by my ambitions and finding those outside of the family circle with whom those ambitions could resonate. My dad was busy keeping the ship afloat and I left the ship to pursue the New York life, occasionally returning to the Minnesota shores.

Dad and I took a taxi to St. Patrick's Cathedral arriving a few minutes before the start of the ceremony. Thousands of people were in attendance. The place was packed and a testament to Bill's influence. I had never been to a Catholic memorial Mass but this one, as someone quipped, was fit for a pope. There were so many members of clergy present that most dioceses in the area would have been hard pressed to offer Mass that day. On the reserved pews were cards that read:

> Reserved Seating
> Memorial Mass
> for the repose of the soul of
> WILLIAM F. BUCKLEY JR.
> St. Patrick's Cathedral
> New York City
> Friday, April 4, 2008
> Ten O'clock

The principal celebrant and homilist was Father George W. Rutler, whom I had met many times at the fortnightly dinners. The Mass included many of the friends and acquaintances I had encountered over the past thirteen years: Linda Bridges, James Buckley, Priscilla Buckley, Trish Buckley, Ed Capano, Jack Fowler, Rich Lowry, Danny Merritt, Jay Nordlinger, James Panero, and Dusty Rhodes, among many others. The eulogists were Henry Kissinger and Christopher Buckley. In his eulogy, Kissinger alluded to the recital I would have given on February 27:

> Even as he participated zestfully in events [in his final years], Bill appeared to be an observer. In the last years, especially in the months before and after Pat's final illness, these moments grew as Bill, beset by illness, seemed to prepare himself for what Christopher has called "his last great voyage." Even then that indomitable spirit never flagged. And he left us working at his desk on a day he had arranged an evening of music surrounded by friends.

Throughout the Mass were musical selections, all chosen by Bill. Bach was featured in the prelude as the guests arrived. There are times when one hears Albinoni's Adagio and wishes it would just go away—but on April 4, played on organ, it penetrated the soul. One of the organists played an improvisation that drove me to tears and seemed an emotional cry for the thousands gathered to mourn Bill's passing and celebrate his life. The waves of sound from the gargantuan organ in St. Patrick's shook everyone, no matter their faith. The Communion Hymn was "Nearer, My God, to Thee" by Sara Adams, from which I think Bill took the title of one of his late books, *Nearer, My God*. In the program book there was a recessional hymn, "I Vow to Thee My Country," by Cecil Spring-Rice, British Ambassador to America from 1912 to 1918, and someone who worked on Britain's behalf to bring America to the battlefields of World War I:

> I vow to thee, my country—all
>   earthly things above—
> Entire and whole and perfect,
>   the service of my love,
> The love that asks no question, the
>   love that stands the test,
> The love that never falters, the
>   love that pays the price.
> The love that makes undaunted
>   the final sacrifice.
> And there's another country I've
>   heard of long ago—
> Most dear to them that love her, most
>   great to them that know,
> We may not count her armies, we
>   may not see her King,
> Her fortress is a faithful heart,
>   her pride is suffering;
> And soul by soul and silently her
>   shining bounds increase,
> And her ways are ways of gentleness,
>   and all her paths are peace.

The Postlude was, fittingly, the valedictory third movement from the Brandenburg Concerto No. 2 by J.S. Bach. Here was the same melody that accompanied Bill as he was beamed into millions of homes week after week and year after year on *Firing Line*. It was as though we had all attended the final episode of Bill's life scripted masterfully by the impresario himself.

Dad and I made our way to the New York Yacht Club where the Who's Who of Bill's life mingled and reminisced. Bringing Dad into the fray with this rarefied world was similar to bringing Mom to Wallacks Point in February. Although Bill was gone, the memoires flourished, and it was an honor to be there with Dad and introduce him to so many friends.

It had been five weeks since Bill's death and it felt like an eternity. I stepped away from the piano for a while as business school concluded and graduation approached. I had to again make decisions about my professional life and next steps in my career. Yet I knew that something was left unfinished. I had never played the Diabelli at the maisonette and Linda had told me back in February before Bill died that he "promises that he'll ask you to do the Diabelli again in the city later in the season, so the rest of us can also hear it!" With the maisonette on the market, I contacted Linda, and she was able to arrange for a recital on July 14, 2008. This would be the recital that never was. She invited Bill's friends who were regulars at my recitals and offered me the opportunity to invite some friends. The list included Priscilla Buckley, *National Review* editors, Charles McGrath and several of my friends including Ann Nadalin, James Panero, Ljova Zhurbin, and business school friends David Disi, Jonathan Garonce and Michael Livanos. We were to have a group of about twenty.

On July 8, Linda wrote "Trish Bozell, one of the siblings you played for back in February, is dying. The doctors are giving her just a few days. So it's entirely possible that Priscilla, who is so enthusiastic about your recital, won't be able to come." Priscilla had attended nearly every recital I had given at the Buckleys' homes. Linda and I discussed whether to postpone, and agreed to proceed and that I would play for Priscilla separately if she couldn't make it. On July 13, Linda wrote, "Just wanted to let you know that Priscilla is definitely coming tomorrow. Trish died yesterday morning, so, as Priscilla put it, all the more reason to do this recital!" I was deeply moved Priscilla would attend under the circumstances and conveyed it to Linda who answered, "My sense of it is that she finds it very fitting—a sort of double tribute."

The recital had the feel of a seance to it and provided closure for me. Priscilla's presence was indeed emotional and as our eyes met there was that feeling of knowing what the other was thinking without saying a word. The fact that I could provide solace for her as she grieved for her sister and remembered her brother was deeply moving for me. In addition to the Diabelli, I started with a Bach Prelude and Fugue and finished with two Liszt transcriptions of Schumann *Lieder*. There's a recording of this recital, which a friend made for my archival purposes. In all of the years I played for Bill there wasn't a single time I recorded one of those fortnightly recitals. This time I didn't pass up the opportunity to capture the performance on the Bösendorfer. It has never been easy for me to listen to my performances, and this one isn't any different. Although mistakes are evident here and there, the unique character of the Buckley piano (Pat's piano!) shines through, and if one listens closely enough one almost hears Bill's exasperation as I tackle the Diabelli one last time. That performance of the Diabelli was indeed my last—I haven't played it since. As the audience of Buckley friends broke up that night, we all knew that this was goodbye to the maisonette. I walked back out onto East 73rd Street to the exact spot where I had first rung the doorbell thirteen years earlier and said farewell to both 73 East 73rd Street and to Bill.

* * *

On the anniversary of Bill's death in February 2009, I wrote to Christopher. I had read his piece in the *Daily Beast* where he marked, in his words, his father's *Yahrzeit*, the Yiddish word for anniversary of a person's death. I reiterated to him just how much I missed his father. He replied with:

> Yes, hard to believe that almost a year ago you were about to put on a concert at Wallack's Point. I have his appointments diary beside me as I type, and the last entry in it, in his impenetrable handwriting, is PERELMAN-CONCERT for the evening of February 27.

Years later I can still imagine Bill that morning as I practiced the Diabelli, sitting and working on his last book, *The Reagan I Knew*. It is only natural that he was writing about his friendship with Ronald Reagan, the man who defeated Communism and whom Bill helped ascend to the presidency. I can see Bill typing and typing, hundreds of words pouring forth from him, as he breathes his last breaths just as the Diabelli, which he so loved, resonates from the Bösendorfer throughout the house at Wallacks Point.

Chapter 23

BUCKLEY'S VIRTUES

My friend Bill had many virtues and those who knew him can each enumerate their own set. These virtues are characteristically American—yet I believe many of them have faded from our society since his death. I learned from Bill before, during, and after knowing him. People are referred to as giants and geniuses, diluting the value of those words, but in Bill's case, those words don't go far enough.

I believe these virtues played a role in shaping Bill so he could contribute to the defeat of one of the great scourges in all of human history: Communism. They also helped him to fight tirelessly against another great scourge: anti-Semitism. This one has again reared its ugly head and seems to be with us for the long haul. Just as Communism was a cancer, so *is* anti-Semitism. Bill's philo-Semitism wasn't as appreciated during his lifetime as his anti-Communism and it deserves to be celebrated today. His actions against both Communism and anti-Semitism were characteristically American. They were the actions of an American impresario to whom I, and our nation, owe a great deal. His virtues played a major role in preparing him for battle against nefarious forces and we as a nation can learn from him and strengthen ourselves for what lies ahead.

Here are some of the virtues that shined brightly for me during our friendship and continue to inspire me to this day:

Communication

Bill was one of the greatest communicators of the twentieth century. From his perch at *National Review* to his fifty-five books to thousands of columns and more than 1,500 episodes of *Firing Line*, he was one of the most prolific writers and personalities in American history. His arrival on the scene coincided with mass media's maturity, especially television. His public speaking engagements took him to countless colleges and universities, along with general speaking engagements, which endeared him to the average person in the flesh. He ran for mayor of New York in 1965, which further propelled his ideas and fame. Bill's tirelessness even led to appearing on sketch-comedy and late-night shows like *Laugh-In and The Tonight Show with Johnny Carson*, respectively. He permeated pop culture to the point that Disney's *Aladdin* released in 1992 included a scene where the character Genie, voiced by Robin Williams, impersonates Bill alongside other pop culture figures including Groucho Marx, Jack Nicholson, Arnold Schwarzenegger, and Ed Sullivan.

Beyond all of these mass communication tools it was "the letter" that was perhaps the most powerful one in Bill's arsenal. Those who knew him were beneficiaries of his letters, and letters formed his core. He wrote tirelessly, maybe dictated even more tirelessly, thousands upon thousands of letters to friends, colleagues, family, strangers, and protégés. If one took the time to write to Bill, he would almost certainly reciprocate. To me this was his ultimate virtue: Beyond the quality of answering the person who wrote a letter to him, Bill respected the time the other person took to write to him. Bill changed lives with his letters. He changed mine and these stories have been told by many others.

Today we live in an age where one mostly writes into an abyss expecting no response and being shocked or heartened by a response. If there is a lesson to learn from Bill and the virtue of communication, it is to respect the time that someone took to write to you since time is the most valuable thing in life. I believe Bill felt a responsibility to answer any letter he received. That is a virtue which today is lacking in the American character: the respect for someone's time, and willingness to write or convey thoughts. Leaving letters and emails unanswered is almost blasphemous but nearly everyone is guilty of this today; leaving the person on the other end questioning why there's no reply. That emptiness and void, silence and selfishness, is something that begins to define a nation and its people.

Many choose not to hear one another today and just talk at one another. The premise of *Firing Line* was two opposing views where people had to hear each other regardless of whether they liked what they heard. This program existed in a three- or four-channel universe when its impact on society far outweighed any comparable program in today's billion-channel universe. We face a reckoning where people who don't agree with each other ignore or cancel each other. This, a nation does not make. Since Bill's death the invisible walls between us have grown higher and higher and I hope we can learn from Bill's prodigious communication skills how to begin to reverse this trend.

Discipline

Bill's discipline was legendary and known to all his friends and colleagues. He was up at 5:00 a.m. and laid down to rest by 10:00 p.m. He would disappear from parties without a trace and knew that every moment beyond the given end time of an event was diminishing in returns. How else could he have accomplished everything he set out to do without the gift of discipline? The multifaceted life which included all of his work platforms also included countless hobbies. Time cannot be manufactured, but through discipline it can be bent and manipulated. This is what Bill did and our society benefited from this discipline. Without it he might have excelled at a few things, but he never could have built the movement and the following he had.

From where did this discipline spring? I believe that a major element was rooted in Bill's quest to become as accomplished a musician as possible. This was forced upon Bill and his siblings at Great Elm, their home in Sharon, Connecticut. He was one of the more gifted Bill children and he dedicated himself to practicing piano in order to try to recreate the musical world that he heard in his mind. The discipline required to master an instrument is similar to that required in sports: focus, determination, and endurance. It's not a coincidence that many successful people also excel in playing musical instruments or sports. At the core of it all lies discipline, without which nothing can be achieved, for even the immensely talented can squander it all without discipline.

Our society has become less disciplined in nearly every area and we see the corrosive effects of this. America has always been defined by discipline. To see it wither away—from our infrastructure to our educational standards—is cause for concern. A return to discipline would strengthen the American character tremendously.

Patriotism

Bill's patriotism was genuine and didn't rely on party labels. For his entire professional life, he was known as the founder of modern-day conservatism. He didn't shy away from that distinction but sometimes also referred to himself as a libertarian, as he did in the subtitle of his book *Happy Days Were Here Again: Reflections of a Libertarian Journalist*. Bill's patriotism was real, and he didn't part ways with those he revered, such as Reagan, when they deviated from the *National Review* line. He understood that governing required compromise and that winning the war against Communism was more important than some of the battles along the way. Conservatism could only become a governing ideology if the majority identified as such, so enforcing orthodoxy did not a patriot make. Instead, building coalitions ruled the day and defined his style of patriotism. Disagreeing with the ideas of the opposition was patriotic. Having friends in the opposition was patriotic.

Our nation is fractured and split between bitter factions. Patriotism is questioned on all sides without respect for each person's right to have a differing point of view. The virtue of patriotism is slipping away from our society, and along with it, American values and how they are perceived by both our population and the world at large. A return to genuine patriotism where one is proud of the country's place in history and contributions to civilization is needed more than ever. It has slipped since Bill's death and we could all benefit from believing in our country and holding those beliefs close to our hearts.

Philanthropy

When one thinks of philanthropy in America, one thinks BIG! Millions or billions given away to charitable causes. This is an incredible American virtue and stands solidly in the American psyche. What is missing today is an anonymous philanthropy where the one who is giving does so without expecting any recognition in return. This is a virtue that is escaping our society with the benefits of philanthropy being the deification of those who give. There is nothing wrong with recognizing those who give, but the overt expectation on the part of celebrity philanthropists to personally benefit from their giving is anathema to real philanthropy.

Bill was an anonymous philanthropist who gave without any expectation of public acknowledgement. Moreover, his style of giving was focused on the individual, either paying for school tuition for the child of a *National Review* staffer or giving a gift to a friend that could prove transformative. His actions were many but no one knows the true number since most have not spoken of those actions. What I have written in the preceding pages is a testament to this man's greatness and what we can learn from his actions, and how we can build upon his example to improve our society.

Transcendent Values

Bill's Catholicism was as well-known as his conservatism. If Bill was a coin, these would likely be the two sides. The values he had were born at Great Elm and were instilled by his family surroundings. His religion came from his mother and he was among the most devout of his siblings. The transcendent values that Bill practiced were part of his credo and those around him benefited from his devoutness.

There were definitely those who lifted an eyebrow when I mentioned my friendship with Bill. That's the thing: It was likely in spite of his religion, which contributed to his immense character, that we became friends. And that is what is extraordinary about his character.

Since Bill's passing, we have continued to see the decline of the importance of transcendent values. A return to these values—whether religious or spiritual in nature—will benefit our nation in myriad ways.

Passing the Torch

As the ultimate showman with immaculate timing, Bill knew when to leave the stage. He was a raconteur who could spar with the best of them and he knew not to stay a moment longer than needed. Bill announced his retirement as editor of *National Review* in 1990 on the eve of his 65th birthday. He retired as host of *Firing Line* in 1999. He subsequently retired from public speaking and even sold his shares in *National Review*. Bill knew when to let go, but more than anything he knew when to let the next generation go forward. This is a virtue that takes immense courage and Bill's ability to pass the torch enabled others to lead. To say that this virtue is in short supply today would be an understatement of monumental proportions. It's not that the advent of longevity requires those of a certain age to retire. But what Bill did was to pave the way for his protégés to have their day in the sun. Bill knew that giving others an opportunity, much like others had given him, would only make his legacy stronger.

America is in need of this virtue. Those who lead must think of the next generation of leadership and give them a chance to see their visions come to fruition. Instead we are watching a constant state of inertia which is a result of a leadership class unwilling to part with power.

Friendship

This is the ultimate virtue. Bill was the consummate friend and would do anything for his friends. He had multitudes and they reciprocated. He was making friends late into life and I was a beneficiary of this virtue. Did he need another friend? Just as others would be winding down or tapped out with friends and not looking for more of them, Bill continued adding friends and building those bonds. This is what Bill mastered throughout his life, and the bonds that he built continue to forge relationships to this day.

Bill had a rare gift, simultaneously exuding charm, warmth, chivalry and friendship. Peter Travers, chairman of National Review Institute, pointed out that Bill treated everyone with respect, whether that person was a train conductor or a maestro. Bill was an everyman at his core even though the persona he evoked seemed patrician to the outside. His run for mayor of New York in 1965 appealed more to the working class than the elites, which seemed counterintuitive to many at the time but became clearer as one understood his aspirational appeal.

Friendship has become secondary to virtual friendship in our society. Conversations and exchange of ideas have been truncated into texts and chats on messenger apps. A phone call is a rarity, let alone getting together without the interference of a technological device. We as a society are drifting farther and farther apart even though we think we're constantly "in touch." We need to return to communication that is direct and even at times foreign to us since we are so removed from personal inter-action. Bill was a masterful friend and host with his wife. They created one of the most beautiful salons in New York where friends would meet, listen to music, and exchange ideas. Events of this kind have become rarer and rarer in our society, replaced by virtual experiences. In order for our society to strengthen we need to return to friendship as a core virtue.

This virtue defined America for its allies, and as we return to personal friendships, we may just find the strengthening of society itself.

Chapter 24

AMERICAN IMPRESARIO

Bill's death was a personal loss for me, and also a deep loss for America. His virtues, especially that of his character, and that of his generation's, made our country cohesive and united, even with the challenges it faced. America's virtues have deteriorated since his generation began to pass away. The sense of community, cordiality, civilized conversation and debate, culture, faith, patriotism, and American homogeneity has been lost. Bill was the soul of American conservatism, and through that helped to shape the American character. Many of Bill's virtues have become a shadow of themselves. Our American character has been diluted, and extremism is more prevalent than ever.

Nearly every time I emailed Bill he would write back within hours or a few days. It might have been a pithy five-word reply, but it was a reply. He was one of the busiest people yet made the time to reply to everyone who wrote to him. He felt a responsibility to answer if someone wrote. How many people were emailing Bill? If he could find time, then anyone can find time.

Each one of Bill's actions and virtues recounted in the preceding pages add up to a man of immense character. His first letter to me in 1994 gave me so much belief in myself, in him, and in humanity. It was only an invitation to play piano for him, but it reverberated within me at the age of eighteen and gave me an incredible amount of confidence. It has been a framed fixture in my life since then and reminds me of my good fortune to have found a kindred spirit in Bill.

To this day I ask myself if the way I met Bill could happen today. I'm not so sure. I hope that those reading this book will look inwards and outwards. Inwards, to see what they can offer the younger generation, and outwards, to find protégés who can benefit from their experiences. I want both to find it within themselves to communicate, write, and reply because without that, nothing will happen.

Bill's reply to my first letter is a lesson for any person who doesn't answer a young person's letter. Let's say you prefer not to meet with the letter writer: Just write back with a decline. That, in and of itself, might teach the recipient a valuable lesson that you're not interested in the topic of their letter rather than leaving them without an answer. Perhaps the fit isn't right, and you have nothing to offer him or her. I received many rejection letters when I was growing up. I kept trying and trying with each letter. However, if you choose to answer and meet the young person then remember how he or she is looking at you through those youthful eyes. Think about what they are experiencing along with their dreams and aspirations. The older we get the more jaded we might become; but try to remember what it was like for you to have that first encounter with someone you revered, respected, and idolized. When I met Bill for the first time in 1995, the experience stayed with me for three-and-a-half years until I met him again. It's doubtful he thought about me a single time except for a fleeting moment when he read my update letters during those intervening years. What's extraordinary is how often I thought of that one day in 1995. The hundreds of times I recounted the experience to family, friends, and complete strangers. My weaving the tale of how Bill replied to my letter and invited me to play piano not only reinforced his humanity and character but also represented something very American. Imagine having hundreds, thousands, or tens of thousands of young people recounting such experiences. This reverberates throughout a nation and inspires others to do the same.

To young people who doubt themselves and think no one will reply to their letter, my experience is an example of a letter changing the entire course of a life. I took the time to write to Bill, so he wrote back. If one person doesn't reply, then follow up. If the person still doesn't reply, then move on to the next person. Don't let it discourage you. The person who doesn't reply to your letter doesn't possess the qualities you're looking for in a mentor. Moreover, he or she took your letter for granted, if they read it all. If they actually read your letter where you expressed your dreams, aspiration, and desires, but still didn't think to acknowledge your time in doing so, this tells you volumes about the person's character. How can a person of dignity and character read a letter from a young person, or any generation, and not reply? It doesn't require the recipient of the letter to make any commitment at all. It doesn't call upon the recipient to agree to meet with the person. What it does require is a reply. For one day the person who doesn't reply to the letter received will themselves write a letter and expect a reply. That is disingenuous and implies a hierarchy that shouldn't exist in the correspondence between people who are created equal.

This gets to the crux of the matter and why I am dwelling on the very act of replying to a letter and the importance of communication. Bill, as the American impresario, created an atmosphere within his ecosystem where communication was paramount. Everyone who knew him will attest to this and how it was one of his most important qualities. The Yale University Library, which houses his archives, received more than a thousand boxes of correspondence attesting to Bill's place as one of the most prolific letter writers of twentieth-century and early twenty-first-century America. He retained copies of both the incoming and outgoing letters. When I was researching this book and missing a few letters, the Yale University Library staff kindly searched some boxes for correspondence between Bill and me. They found many of the letters I wrote to him; with the exception of the very first one, which seems to have been misplaced and might be in another one of the hundreds of boxes. Perhaps it is fate that that first letter was lost—but only after he had a chance to read it!

Three-and-a-half years elapsed between the time I played for Bill in April 1995 and when we met again in November of 1998. He kindly replied to my updates, which kept my youthful exuberance, well, exuberant. However, everything changed with my letter to him after college graduation in 1998. This one piqued his interest and Bill must have decided that I was protégé material and that he was interested in becoming a guiding light for me. I had November 2, 1998, on my calendar for two months, and Bill already knew for those two months that he was going to offer me a grant! He had a plan. I didn't know anything about his plan but there was already a level of trust between us. Bill saw something in me, but more important than that, Bill wanted to do this. I didn't ask him for a grant. I didn't go to him with hat in hand. I simply wrote him a letter where I declared boldly that I wanted to do for classical music what he had done for conservatism in America. It seems to have resonated in such a powerful way that upon reading my letter, around the time of his lunch with Schuyler Chapin, he already decided that I would help him to answer the question "What does the lack of art cost you?" It's remarkable to me that analyzing this twenty-six years later, I see just how great this man was and how much it says about his character. There I sat in the Red Room in the maisonette on 73rd and Park Avenue, speaking with Bill, and he already knew that he was going to offer me the grant. He knew he was going to take a first-generation American, child of Soviet Jewish immigrants, and give him a transformative opportunity. This took trust, character, and belief in the future.

Richard Brookhiser wrote in *Right Time, Right Place* about Bill's generosity. After purchasing a second home in 1999 in the eastern Catskills, Brookhiser mentioned to Bill that it would require some work in order to "bring it up to snuff." Bill came to the rescue. Brookhiser writes:

> Three months after we bought it [the second home], I got a letter from Bill (hand addressed, so as to escape even Frances's notice), with a check for ten thousand dollars: "I am very pleased for you and Jeanie that your dream-house is abuilding. I want to make a contribution to it—the winterization you spoke of—in memory of a long friendship, done with great affection.

Bill always had trouble with proper names, never with the big gesture. I was hardly alone in receiving these gifts—without making any effort, I learned of many: a plane ticket for Harry Jaffa so he could fly east to see his son graduate from college; help with Ed Capano's first mortgage...there were many more such gifts, but Bill's biographer will have to be diligent to uncover them; he did not tell disinterested parties, much less his left hand.

The gifts that Bill bestowed on me mirror many of the acts described by Brookhiser. There was the research grant itself, the honoraria for the recitals, the reception following my thirtieth-birthday recital, the $10,000 gift in 2007, and the offer to fly me back to New York to play for him in the months after Pat's death. It was also rumored, among those close to Bill, that he had paid for the Catholic school education for children of his staff, including his maids. Bill spoke Spanish with his Spanish-speaking housekeepers, who in turn referred to him as *Padre* because he treated and respected them like family. There was warmth between Bill and Pat and those who worked for them for decades. The generosity came naturally, with no strings attached.

However, far greater than any financial gifts, was the trust, friendship and time he gave those around him. Most valuable were the lessons we all learned from Bill's humanity.

As we grow older, we realize that the value of time increases since we have less of it. Each year, month, day, hour, minute, and second increases in value as each second, minute, hour, day, month, and year passes. Bill's generosity increased each day of our friendship as we spent more and more time together. His generosity with time was only possible through his extraordinary discipline.

One of my oldest friends, both literally and figuratively, is the brilliant British businessman Brian Beazer; we met in Switzerland during the European tour I produced in 1997. Now eighty-nine, over the years, Brian has often spoken with me about the value of time. At eighty-five he made a short video entitled "Keys to a Life Well-Lived" for his eponymous company and one can still find it on YouTube. In it he eloquently explains that "use of time and self-discipline" are two of the most important elements in life:

> One of the great things in life is not to waste any time. If you live a very long life…you will live a maximum of 900,000 hours, that's all any of us have, so don't waste any of them. Now, you can spend money today, but tomorrow you can earn some more. But if you spend time today, you can't earn anymore tomorrow. So, making the best use of your time…is of the greatest importance. And then I think, in the use of time, a great issue is self-discipline. If you're not self-disciplined and you say, "Well, I'll lie in bed until 10:00 this morning, etc.," you have to bear in mind that you're using up part of those 900,000 hours, so it's important that you have self-discipline to push you out to play tennis, go shopping or whatever else you want to do. So, I think that use of time and self-discipline are very important to us at

all ages, but especially when you're over fifty-five...you've already used 600,000 of those
900,000 hours.

Bill was sixty-nine when we met in 1995, and I was nineteen.
To imagine that he shared with me so many of the remaining
hours he had left was an incredible act of generosity. To build
on Brian's point, Bill was one of the most disciplined people I
have ever met, and I think all his friends would agree. He was
up at 5:00 a.m. and would leave evening events unannounced
to get to bed, knowing that each late-night hour, at least for
him, meant diminishing returns the next day. This kept him at
the top of his game into his later years, powering his prodigious
output of articles, books, meetings, hobbies, and so much more.

That discipline was a virtue of Bill's that his friends and
acquaintances knew well. He was a master at working a room
and getting to the point. A conversation with him at a party
was like a flash of lightning. He would focus in on you with the
grin, a "hey, buddy," a couple of pleasantries and questions, and
before you knew it he was on to the next person. He knew he
had to be efficient to accomplish so much in a lifetime: Editing
and running *National Review*, writing thousands of letters and
columns, authoring dozens of books, hosting *Firing Line*, giving speechs, engaging in his many hobbies like sailing and, of
course, playing the piano and harpsichord. Let's not forget the
countless friendships and the protégés he mentored.

Our society has shifted in the other direction, with more
and more time wasted (whether on social media or through
consumption of endless headlines) and less discipline. This has
shifted the focus to trivial matters over substantive ones. Depth
of thought and commitment to education has diminished and
with it engagement with one another. Bill's engagement with

me and his decision to become my mentor was the epitome of generosity. If we all became more attuned to the value of time and began to give some of our time to the younger generation, we would find more meaning and discipline in our lives, and begin to strengthen our society's foundation.

William F. Buckley, Jr., left enormous shoes to fill, and sixteen years on they are as empty as they were after he passed away. His passing didn't destabilize our society's equilibrium, yet the loss of this American impresario has led to a blurred vision for this country. His ability to produce—whether the written word, a television program, or even a recital—were all part of his vision for his America. We still have his memory and his wisdom through his boundless contributions.

This book is my testament to William F. Buckley, Jr., and I hope that you, the reader, have come away with a renewed appreciation for this great man and how we can all benefit from emulating the elements of his character. I am eternally grateful for everything he did for our country and for what I learned from this friend, mentor, hero, and American impresario. Thank you, Bill.

Epilogue

THE BÖSENDORFER

After Bill passed away, in addition to the maisonette being put up for sale, many of the Buckleys' belonging were going to be auctioned at Christie's. I wondered what would happen with the Bösendorfer on which I had played so many times. In December 2010, I wrote to Linda Bridges enquiring about the piano, and she forwarded me an email from Christopher indicating that I could contact Christie's about the piano. I thought it was a stretch, buying the Buckley piano. Nevertheless, I wrote to Christie's, and to my surprise this iconic instrument dating back to 1927 was being offered to me, courtesy of Christopher's generosity, for $5,000. The market value of a new Bösendorfer of similar dimensions would have been far north of $100,000. This was a priceless instrument and played a central role in the Buckleys' lives for many decades. In April 2011, I purchased the Bösendorfer, but left it in storage since it couldn't fit it in my apartment. For years it stayed in storage until I had it refurbished in 2017. Since early 2020, the Buckley Bösendorfer has resided at a friend's home in Princeton, New Jersey, on loan until my family and I have a home large enough for it. Every time I visit and play it, I remember the fortnightly dinners and Bill's joy at hearing "good music."

Acknowledgments

Thank you to my wife Anna for supporting me during the time it took to write this book. There were many nights and weekends when I had to disappear for hours to write. Although she never met William F. Buckley, Jr., by now, she knows him well, and he would have loved her. My daughters Elizabeth and Gabriella are too young to understand the ideas in this book, but I do hope that one day they will read it and come away with a better understanding of their family, father, and his friend, Bill. I've told Elizabeth, nearly five, about Bill from time to time and referred to him simply as "Buckley." Recently when I came home, she asked, "Papa, were you with your friend Buckley?" I smiled and wished that had been the case.

Thank you to Christopher Buckley for giving his "blessing" to the idea of this book, permission to use the photographs and materials related to his father, and giving me access to the Buckley archives at the Beinecke Rare Book & Manuscript Library at Yale University. Thank you to the librarians for searching for, and retrieving, copies of correspondence.

Thank you to Jack Fowler, former publisher of *National Review*, for kindly introducing me to my publisher. I wrote to

Jack about my idea for a book celebrating William F. Buckley, Jr. and never expected it to become a reality.

Thank you to David Bernstein, publisher of Bombardier Books, for the opportunity to write this book, my first book, as well as for his guidance throughout the process. His insight was invaluable and gave me the confidence to broaden the thesis from what I originally envisaged as a memoir of my friendship with Bill.

Thank you to Aleigha Koss and the entire team at Post Hill Press.

Thank you to Karina Rollins, my copy editor, for her brilliant work and suggestions.

Thank you to James Panero for reading the manuscript and giving me some incredible insight days before the manuscript was due.

Thank you to Mom and Dad for rekindling many childhood memories, providing family history, and details on immigrating to America.

Thank you to my brother Rubin for markedly improving my writing style in high school.

Thank you to *National Review* and National Review Institute, especially Peter Travers and Lindsay Craig, for their friendship and for several important introductions along the way.

Thank you to Lauren Noble and the Buckley Institute in New Haven, Connecticut.

Thank you to the Hoover Institution for making available numerous photographs from relevant episodes of *Firing Line*, including the photograph on the cover of this book.

Thank you to Richard Brookhiser and Jay Nordlinger for refreshing my memory of evenings with the Buckleys.

Posthumously, thank you to Linda Bridges for her friendship and for being the great connector to Bill in his final years.

In addition to William F. Buckley, Jr., I have been blessed with a group of mentors, one of whom is David Bell, the legendary advertising executive. Thank you for tweaking the title and encouraging me to select an image from *Firing Line* for the cover.

In addition to those in the main body of the book, I would like to thank some of the people who have played important roles in my life before, during and/or after my friendship with Bill, including John Abeles; Lidia Bastianich; Fiorenza and Yoron Cohen; Christopher Foley; Roger Forsberg; Sir Clive Gillinson; Scott Goldshine; Isabelle Harnoncourt-Feigen; Sumita Kumar; Gianandrea and Lucia Noseda; David W. Packard; Linda Passon-McNally; Maya Pritsker; Vladimir and Svetlana Rabinstein; Larry, Carol, Adam, and Andrea Saper; Sir David Scholey; R. Douglas Sheldon; Jacqueline Singer; Helga Rabl-Stadler; Ettore Volontieri; and posthumously, Mitch Leigh and Richard Snyder.

Thank you to those reading this book. I hope you enjoyed it.

Lawrence Perelman
New York City
September 2024

About the Author

Lawrence Perelman is founder and CEO of Semantix Creative Group, a strategic advisory firm specializing in business strategy, management, and PR/ Communications for a wide range of artists, institutions, and companies in the performing arts. He has advised some of the greatest artists in the world, including conductor Gianandrea Noseda, violinist Anne-Sophie Mutter, pianist Martha Argerich, as well as the legendary Salzburg Festival for over two decades. He is also a co-founder and business strategy consultant at Carnegie Hall+, a performing arts streaming service. He is a native of St. Paul, Minnesota and studied to become a concert pianist. He attended Manhattan School of Music and graduated from Macalester College with a BA in Political Science and Music. He holds an MBA from Columbia Business School. He resides in New York with his wife and two daughters.

Photography Credit: Stefano Pasqualetti